Llewellyn's

Witches' Datebook

2012

Featuring

Art by Jennifer Hewitson
Text by Elizabeth Barrette, Deborah Blake,
Tabitha Bradley, Dallas Jennifer Cobb,
Ellen Dugan, Sybil Fogg, James Kambos,
Kristin Madden, and Sharynne MacLeod NicMhacha

ISBN 978-0-7387-1213-0

2012

JANUARY
S	M	T	W	T	F	S
1	2	3	4	5	6	7
8	9	10	11	12	13	14
15	16	17	18	19	20	21
22	23	24	25	26	27	28
29	30	31				

FEBRUARY
S	M	T	W	T	F	S
			1	2	3	4
5	6	7	8	9	10	11
12	13	14	15	16	17	18
19	20	21	22	23	24	25
26	27	28	29			

MARCH
S	M	T	W	T	F	S
				1	2	3
4	5	6	7	8	9	10
11	12	13	14	15	16	17
18	19	20	21	22	23	24
25	26	27	28	29	30	31

APRIL
S	M	T	W	T	F	S
1	2	3	4	5	6	7
8	9	10	11	12	13	14
15	16	17	18	19	20	21
22	23	24	25	26	27	28
29	30					

MAY
S	M	T	W	T	F	S
		1	2	3	4	5
6	7	8	9	10	11	12
13	14	15	16	17	18	19
20	21	22	23	24	25	26
27	28	29	30	31		

JUNE
S	M	T	W	T	F	S
					1	2
3	4	5	6	7	8	9
10	11	12	13	14	15	16
17	18	19	20	21	22	23
24	25	26	27	28	29	30

JULY
S	M	T	W	T	F	S
1	2	3	4	5	6	7
8	9	10	11	12	13	14
15	16	17	18	19	20	21
22	23	24	25	26	27	28
29	30	31				

AUGUST
S	M	T	W	T	F	S
			1	2	3	4
5	6	7	8	9	10	11
12	13	14	15	16	17	18
19	20	21	22	23	24	25
26	27	28	29	30	31	

SEPTEMBER
S	M	T	W	T	F	S
						1
2	3	4	5	6	7	8
9	10	11	12	13	14	15
16	17	18	19	20	21	22
23	24	25	26	27	28	29
30						

OCTOBER
S	M	T	W	T	F	S
	1	2	3	4	5	6
7	8	9	10	11	12	13
14	15	16	17	18	19	20
21	22	23	24	25	26	27
28	29	30	31			

NOVEMBER
S	M	T	W	T	F	S
				1	2	3
4	5	6	7	8	9	10
11	12	13	14	15	16	17
18	19	20	21	22	23	24
25	26	27	28	29	30	

DECEMBER
S	M	T	W	T	F	S
						1
2	3	4	5	6	7	8
9	10	11	12	13	14	15
16	17	18	19	20	21	22
23	24	25	26	27	28	29
30	31					

2013

JANUARY
S	M	T	W	T	F	S
		1	2	3	4	5
6	7	8	9	10	11	12
13	14	15	16	17	18	19
20	21	22	23	24	25	26
27	28	29	30	31		

FEBRUARY
S	M	T	W	T	F	S
					1	2
3	4	5	6	7	8	9
10	11	12	13	14	15	16
17	18	19	20	21	22	23
24	25	26	27	28		

MARCH
S	M	T	W	T	F	S
					1	2
3	4	5	6	7	8	9
10	11	12	13	14	15	16
17	18	19	20	21	22	23
24	25	26	27	28	29	30
31						

APRIL
S	M	T	W	T	F	S
	1	2	3	4	5	6
7	8	9	10	11	12	13
14	15	16	17	18	19	20
21	22	23	24	25	26	27
28	29	30				

MAY
S	M	T	W	T	F	S
			1	2	3	4
5	6	7	8	9	10	11
12	13	14	15	16	17	18
19	20	21	22	23	24	25
26	27	28	29	30	31	

JUNE
S	M	T	W	T	F	S
						1
2	3	4	5	6	7	8
9	10	11	12	13	14	15
16	17	18	19	20	21	22
23	24	25	26	27	28	29
30						

JULY
S	M	T	W	T	F	S
	1	2	3	4	5	6
7	8	9	10	11	12	13
14	15	16	17	18	19	20
21	22	23	24	25	26	27
28	29	30	31			

AUGUST
S	M	T	W	T	F	S
				1	2	3
4	5	6	7	8	9	10
11	12	13	14	15	16	17
18	19	20	21	22	23	24
25	26	27	28	29	30	31

SEPTEMBER
S	M	T	W	T	F	S
1	2	3	4	5	6	7
8	9	10	11	12	13	14
15	16	17	18	19	20	21
22	23	24	25	26	27	28
29	30					

OCTOBER
S	M	T	W	T	F	S
		1	2	3	4	5
6	7	8	9	10	11	12
13	14	15	16	17	18	19
20	21	22	23	24	25	26
27	28	29	30	31		

NOVEMBER
S	M	T	W	T	F	S
					1	2
3	4	5	6	7	8	9
10	11	12	13	14	15	16
17	18	19	20	21	22	23
24	25	26	27	28	29	30

DECEMBER
S	M	T	W	T	F	S
1	2	3	4	5	6	7
8	9	10	11	12	13	14
15	16	17	18	19	20	21
22	23	24	25	26	27	28
29	30	31				

Llewellyn's Witches' Datebook 2012 © 2011 by Llewellyn Worldwide, 2143 Wooddale Dr., Dept. 978-0-7387-1213-0, Woodbury, MN 55125-2989. All rights reserved. No part of this publication may be reproduced in any form without the permission of the publisher, except for quotations used in critical reviews. Llewellyn is a registered trademark of Llewellyn Worldwide Ltd.

Editing/design by Ed Day

Cover illustration and interior art © 2011 by Jennifer Hewitson

Art on chapter openings © 2006 by Jennifer Hewitson

Cover design by Anne Marie Garrison

Table of Contents

How to Use *Llewellyn's Witches' Datebook* 4
Dark of the Moon *by Ellen Dugan* 6
The Mystic Tray *by Sybil Fogg* 10
Timecraft: Temporal Spellwork *by Elizabeth Barrette* 14
Candle Magic *by James Kambos* 19
Scrapbooking Your BOS *by Tabitha Bradley* 24
January 29
February 38
March 46
April 55
May 64
June 72
July 81
August 90
September 99
October 108
November 116
December 125
About the Authors 136
Appendix 138
Notes 142

How to Use Llewellyn's Witches' Datebook

Welcome to *Llewellyn's Witches' Datebook 2012!* This datebook was designed especially for Witches, Pagans, and magical people. Use it to plan sabbat celebrations, magic, Full Moon rites, and even dentist and doctor appointments. At right is a symbol key to some of the features of this datebook.

MOON QUARTERS: The Moon's cycle is divided into four quarters, which are noted in the calendar pages along with their exact times. When the Moon changes quarter, both quarters are listed, as well as the time of the change. In addition, a symbol for the new quarter is placed where the numeral for the date usually appears.

MOON IN THE SIGNS: Approximately every two and a half days, the Moon moves from one zodiac sign to the next. The sign that the Moon is in at the beginning of the day (midnight Eastern Time) is noted next to the quarter listing. If the Moon changes signs that day, there will be a notation saying "☽ enters" followed by the symbol for the sign it is entering.

MOON VOID-OF-COURSE: Just before the Moon enters a new sign, it will make one final aspect (angular relationship) to another planet. Between that last aspect and the entrance of the Moon into the next sign it is said to be void-of-course. Activities begun when the Moon is void-of-course rarely come to fruition, or they turn out very differently than planned.

PLANETARY MOVEMENT: When a planet or asteroid moves from one sign into another, this change (called an *ingress*) is noted on the calendar pages with the exact time. The Moon and Sun are considered planets in this case. The planets (except for the Sun and Moon) can also appear to move backward as seen from the Earth. This is called a *planetary retrograde*, and is noted on the calendar pages with the symbol ℞. When the planet begins to move forward, or direct, again, it is marked D, and the time is also noted.

PLANTING AND HARVESTING DAYS: The best days for planting and harvesting are noted on the calendar pages with a seedling icon (planting) and a basket icon (harvesting).

TIME ZONE CHANGES: The times and dates of all astrological phenomena in this datebook are based on Eastern time. If you live outside the Eastern time zone, you will need to make the following changes: Pacific Time subtract three hours; Mountain Time subtract two hours; Central Time subtract one hour; Alaska subtract four hours; and Hawaii subtract five hours. All data is adjusted for Daylight Saving Time.

Planets

☉	Sun	♆	Neptune
☽	Moon	♇	Pluto
☿	Mercury	⚷	Chiron
♀	Venus	⚳	Ceres
♂	Mars	⚴	Pallas
♃	Jupiter	⚵	Juno
♄	Saturn	⚶	Vesta
♅	Uranus		

Signs

♈	Aries	♐	Sagittarius
♉	Taurus	♑	Capricorn
♊	Gemini	♒	Aquarius
♋	Cancer	♓	Pisces
♌	Leo		

Motion

℞	Retrograde
D	Direct

♍	Virgo		
♎	Libra		
♏	Scorpio		

1st Quarter/New Moon ☽   3rd Quarter/Full Moon ☺
2nd Quarter ☽   4th Quarter ☽

☽ **Tuesday** ←——— Day and date
1st ♎ ←——————— Moon's quarter and sign
2nd Quarter 4:01 am ←——— Moon quarter change   Planting day →
☽ v/c 4:01 am ←——————— Moon void-of-course
☽ enters ♏ 9:30 am ←——— Moon sign change/ingress
♄ ℞ 10:14 am ←
Color: Gray ←——————— Planetary retrograde   Harvesting day →
               Color of the day

Dark
of the Moon
by Ellen Dugan

One of my favorite coven gatherings and solitary magickal celebrations is a "Dark of the Moon" ritual. Why? Well, because they are *different*. The energy is more intense, and the magick tends to be a touch more dramatic, personal, and powerful. Sure, working at the Full Moon or gathering a coven together at that time is both a time-honored and classic way to celebrate ... but you may want to consider tossing a couple Dark of the Moon celebrations into the mix. You'll be surprised at the difference in the energy and the intensity of the magick.

Technically, the Dark of the Moon is the time when there is "no solar reflection" on the Moon. As the light from the Sun is completely behind the Moon during this time, the Moon appears dark to us here on earth. This "dark" phase lasts for about three days, until that superslim, waxing crescent Moon appears low in the western skies just after sunset.

The astronomical New Moon is sometimes referred to as the *Dark Moon* to avoid confusion. The New Moon *is* the moment the Sun and Moon become conjunct, which is the time often listed on calendars.

However, the "Dark of the Moon phase" in regard to spellcasting is defined less rigidly. The two days before, and the day of the New Moon are classically identified as the "Dark Moon phase." On these three enchanting days, you have a chance to flex your magickal muscles and to learn a little something new about yourself and your Craft.

When I first began studying the Craft many years ago, I was told that the Dark of the Moon was a magickal time best avoided. To which my answer is *"Pffft."* I'm here to tell you that notion is simply ridiculous. I enjoy working during all lunar phases, but I have to admit there is something extra appealing about a Dark Moon ritual, spell, or celebration for clearing out emotional and psychic clutter, removing negativity, and making room for new beginnings.

I have always found that during the Dark of the Moon, my psychic abilities are turned up to full blast. My instincts are better and I can direct and harness magickal energy just as easily as during a Full Moon. This is because during this dark lunar phase, all energies are typically turned inward (and that goes for everybody), which is perfect for transformation and clearing out what is no longer needed—a bad habit, a negative person in your life. Is something or someone holding you back or making you feel down? This is the time to remove such obstacles from your path. So take stock, and release what is no longer needed.

With the psychic focus turned upon yourself and your own emotions and thoughts, the Dark of the Moon phase is the perfect occasion for soul-searching, reflection, deep meditation, and accessing your shadow side. We all have a darker side, so take this time to get to know it, come to terms with it, and to embrace it. Doing so will help you regain confidence and build up your psychic, magickal, and emotional strength.

This type of magick packs a punch! This is the Crone's lunar phase, a prime time to connect with deities such as the Morrigan, Lilith, Cerridwen, Nepthys, or Hecate. If you want to learn something new, to challenge yourself, and push your own boundaries a bit, this is the way to go. However, you will need a few things before you begin working magick during the Dark of the Moon. Oh, and I'm betting that you already possess them.

These "things" are actually personality traits. You have to have courage, confidence, and self-control to work rituals and magick during the dark of the Moon. Scaredy Witches need not apply. So let's break it down and take a look at these magickal requirements.

Courage: No fear. There is no place for fear in the Craft. If you are working your magick for personal transformation and you allow fear to creep into the mix, you are smothering the spell and putting limits on its manifestations in the physical world. Be businesslike. Wild swings in your mood or casting when you are angry or upset is the utmost in stupidity. Ground and center and be cool. This is the point where you do have to pull up your "Big Witch" panties (or briefs, as the case may be) and deal. If you can't stay calm and focused, then you shouldn't be directing powerful magicks out and about anyway—in any lunar phase!

Confidence: Study, knowledge, and experience are what build confidence. It always makes me smile to hear a Witch say, "I've been a practicing Witch for (so many) years. I'm practicing until I get it right!" You will always be a student of the magickal arts. This is a life-long study, or as I have heard it described, "a permanent, on the job, magickal training." It is both exciting and fun! Keep pushing, studying, and experimenting with your Craft. See where it takes you and find out what your specialties are. Discovering your individual psychic strengths and magickal talents builds confidence. Explore your own talents and keep building up your strengths. Look at it this way: it takes exercise, effort, and repetition to build up a stronger muscle. Magick is definitely like any other muscle. You do have to work it to become stronger. This will take dedication and effort. Confidence is built with practice, repetition, and persistence. But if you stick to it, you will be rewarded with poise, making you secure in your own magickal abilities, no matter what the situation. Confidence is a quietly beautiful strength.

Self-control: *With great power comes great responsibility.* That's not just a line from the Spiderman movie. It counts for Witches too. We cart around a lot of magickal and psychic firepower, so we have to

be responsible and to possess self-control. No excuses and no bullcrap. True Witches have worked hard, studied their Craft, and put effort into their daily spiritual practices. These individuals will know their own strengths, and strive to be in control of themselves and their personal powers at all times. Because truthfully, that self-discipline allows any magickal change that is manifested to be smooth, controlled, and beautifully strong—especially during the Dark of the Moon. As at this time our magick is all focused internally. So we will feel the effects of any magicks immediately. Self-control is an exquisite and powerful thing.

Dark of the Moon Spell

Here is a spell for transformation that you can try during the Dark of the Moon.

Supplies: I would suggest lighting black votive candles and placing dark-colored fresh flowers upon your altar. Scatter some star confetti on the work surface or light up your favorite incense. Wear dark purple or black, and allow some quiet, personal time for meditation when the spell is finished.

Don't be afraid to personalize this spell and make it your own! Feel free to add symbols of the things, perceptions, or troublesome people that you need to release from your life. Finally, I would suggest casting this spell at night and outside under the stars. Also, this spell can be easily adapted for a Coven instead of a Solitary working. Just switch out the words "I" for "we," and "my" for "our."

> The Moon is hidden during this powerful time,
> Bring healing and beginnings as I speak this rhyme.
> Oh, Hecate, Lilith, and Cerridwen,
> I call you now, let the magick begin.
> Nepthys and Morrigan, hear my call,
> Bring transformation to one and all.
> The Moon is dark, but magick still whispers through the air,
> I call for change now, with confidence, courage, and flair.
> By shadows and starlight this spell is spun,
> As I will so mote it be an let it harm none.

Allow the candles to burn until they go out on their own. Take the rest of the evening to contemplate the new beginnings and fresh opportunities that await you. Happy Dark of the Moon! Blessed be.

The Mystic Tray
by Sybil Fogg

A couple of years ago, my mother-in-law gave me a Mystic Tray. She had recently moved in with her father and was in the process of helping him clean out his house and would periodically bring us bags of books and interesting antiques.

I had never heard of the Mystic Tray, so the first order of business was to research this cross between a toy and a serving apparatus. The Mystic Tray is a talking board, similar to the more popular Ouija board. As these boards are a means of communicating with the spirit realm, it only seems natural that they find their roots in trance mediums. A trance medium, as the name suggests, is a person who is able to go into a trance and allow his or her body to be taken over by spirits. In this state, spirits, elementals, and/or Fey talk through the medium.

There are other ways a medium may contact the spirit world. One common method is automatic writing, a technique of channeling spirits via pen and paper that was particularly popular during the fad of spiritualism at the turn of the last century. George Hyde-Lees Yeats, the wife of the Irish poet William Butler Yeats, is probably one of the most well-known people with this particular gift. Her writings influenced much of Yeats' poetry and the two of them were heavily involved in the Golden Dawn, a magical order active in Britain during the nineteenth and twentieth centuries. Many believe that the Golden Dawn is the most influential group on modern occultism. Nonetheless, the Golden Dawn is responsible for bringing different means of speaking with the unseen world to the attention of many.

This burgeoning interest in the occult by Victorian society led to a widespread popularity of parlor games involving contacting the spiritual realm. In the beginning, a person would sit with pen and paper and allow ghosts to write through them. To prove that they were not cheating, mediums began to use a small basket containing a writing utensil placed on a piece of paper. The recipient of the message would loosely grasp the pen and allow it to move of its own accord. Later, letters and numbers were written out and a wine glass was placed in the center of the page and moved around by participants until those from the "other side" took over.

The difference between talking boards and automatic writing is, of course, the medium in which contact with the spirits is transferred. A trance medium will allow his or her body to give way to the mystical world and become a portal. The messages received are then recorded on paper. In a similar way, someone using a talking board combines his or her energy with the spiritual realm and together they communicate, but instead of with paper and pen, the medium rests his or her hand on a *planchette* (French for "little plank"), a small wooden board often in a triangular shape supported by little feet. The planchette rests on a board with letters, words, and numbers. The spirit will move this board around to spell out words and phrases usually in response to questions.

In 1891, the "Ouija Board" was patented and marketed. In 1966, Parker Brothers purchased the patent and added the board to its many games already on the market. (www.paralumun.com/ouijaboard.htm)

So, where does the Mystic Tray fit in? Haskelite manufactured the trays in the 1940s (www.museumoftalkingboards.com/history.html). They are based on the Ouija board design, but with slight differences.

This board is similar to the Ouija board, in that the board contains letters, numbers, the necessary "yes" and "no" for quick answers, the "Goodbye" and even a "Hello," and the additional forecast of "Conditions Good."

The differences are apparent right away. This board doubles as a tray with upturned sides. Instead of the common Moon and Sun, there are four pictures: a turban-clad sheik in both the upper left corner and lower right corner, a camel secures his place in the upper right corner, and the Disney witch from "Snow White" harbors the lower left corner. Perhaps this lends credence to the fact that talking boards were once called "witch boards." A transparent sphinx resides in the middle of the board.

Talking boards have been used throughout the centuries as party games and in magical workings by serious practitioners. The first time I attempted to contact the other side with a board was when I was fifteen and visiting my family's farm in 1987. My grandparents had an older Ouija Board and that Christmas Eve, I stole from my bedroom to the parlor with the board. The farm house was the perfect setting for such contact as it was rather ancient and contained many belongings of my ancestors. I figured it would be best to call on them. I had put much thought into the preparations for such contact. I cast a crude circle, sprinkled salt water, and lit candles. Once everything seemed quiet, spooky, and the stage set, I sat with my board, laid my fingers lightly on the planchette, and began to sweep it in figure eights around the board. Unfortunately, as soon as I made contact, I was too tongue-tied to ask any relevant questions. My mother now owns that Ouija Board and I haven't had a chance to work with it since. Throughout the years, I have tried others with varying responses.

As soon as I saw the Mystic Tray, I was overcome with a desire to try it out. After exploring it off and on for a couple of months, I thought it was time to develop a spell around it. This spell is best done at Samhain when the veil between the two worlds is thinnest. It is not necessary to purchase a Mystic Tray, especially as they are not manufactured anymore. It is okay to use a Ouija board or in my opinion, it is more potent to work with one that has been created specifically for this purpose.

Time: The Dark Moon nearest Samhain.

Tools: Talking board placed in the center of the room. Although it is possible to do this magical working at a table, I find it grounding to sit on the floor when I work with a talking board.

- Quarter candles set out in their appropriate places.
- Two center candles to represent the God and Goddess. I usually use a blue candle for the goddess and a green candle for the god, but please use the colors you are most accustomed to.
- Additional candles—black, white, or a color that represents who you want to contact set up around your working space.
- Pictures of the deceased or objects that belonged to them. Lay

this within your working space beyond the talking board. Make sure you can see this, as it will be your focal point.

• Any tools you normally use to cast a circle

Call the Quarters

"Faeries, owls, and spirits taking flight, I request your presence tonight." Light the east candle.

"Salamanders, flames, imps, and light, I request your presence tonight." Light the south candle.

"Nereids, whales, coral, and water sprites, I request your presence tonight." Light the west candle.

"Tree nymphs, trolls, gnomes hear this rite, I request your presence tonight." Light the north candle.

Light the candles for the Goddess and God and request their presence. Cast the circle as you normally would. Light the candles in your circle. Sit and rest your fingers on the planchette. Gaze at your loved one's photo.

Will yourself to relax. I find it helpful to move the planchette around the board. I normally move it in a clockwise circle these days because I am drawing energy to me. If you are more comfortable with the traditional figure eight, then use that. The concept that this movement represents a negative spirit taking over the board is superstition.

When you feel the planchette moving of its own, you have made contact. Ask any questions you have to keep the conversation flowing.

When you are finished with your visit, remember to thank your guest and to blow out your candles and close your circle appropriately.

Channeling is taxing both mentally and physically. I recommend spending time in quiet reflection when you have completed a session. Afterwards, make sure to eat a healthy meal and rest.

For more information, check out: www.museumoftalkingboards.com. Not only will you find a plethora of information regarding talking boards, this site is chock full of humor as well.

Timecraft: Temporal Spellwork
by Elizabeth Barrette

Time manifests in many different ways. In the workaday world, we experience "clock time," which is presented as an objective means of measuring the unvaried flow of moments. As magical practitioners, we experience time as a flexible medium, which we can sometimes alter according to our needs. The more you understand about time, the easier it will be for you to influence.

The Nature of Time

Physics teaches us about the space-time continuum. This is simply the "area" of the physical world that we inhabit, a broad curve of space and time woven together. The space-time continuum supports our bodies and gives our souls a chance to experience life on the material plane.

However, time is also an illusion—especially linear time. We tend to experience time as a one-way flow with three sections: the past, the present, and the future. This illusion springs from our mortality, which is a journey from birth through life to death (and so forth). From this perspective time "looks like" a line. When a soul is not attached to a body, it can perceive time as an area, not a line; the soul can move freely, independent of the individual life-lines or history-lines. In this regard, life is a bit like a temporal gravity well. On the Earth, our bodies stick to the Earth, just as our lives stick to a timeline; but in space, our bodies float weightlessly because gravity has different effects there, just as our disembodied souls are not bound by linear time. Quantum physics even gives us a hint in this direction, because some of its theories suggest that time flows in both directions.

These features of time help determine how we can manipulate it or move ourselves through it. When we shape our awareness of time, we can shape time itself.

Expanding Time

Time is elastic. It can stretch. This is most noticeable when something boring or embarrassing "seems to take forever." People experience this effect often, but if they don't consider it "real," then they can't take advantage of it. Once you realize that it's a valid experience, you can do it on purpose and use this to your advantage.

When you want to stretch time, first decide the sphere. You can create just a subjective bubble, which is ideal for any solitary activity, such as studying, meditation, or sleep. It is much easier to alter time only for yourself. With more experience, you can carry another person (or a few) along for the ride. This is most useful when you have a conversation that will take longer than the objective time you have available. If you're covering someone else, pay extra attention to the boundaries: you can only affect a small area, so it's best to look for a natural marker, such as the walls of a room or edge of a clearing. Remember that you'll be out of phase with consensus reality, so if someone comes looking for you they may not find you.

There are different techniques for stretching time. One relies on its inherent elasticity. You can get a more precise effect ("I want to study for three hours, but I only have one on the clock") because you're doing it by hand, and it's easier to let go of quickly. It's also more work to grab time with your mind and stretch it bigger. When you do this, think not just of stretching, but of the feeling you get when time seems to drag; that's what you're aiming to create. Another method is to sidestep our timestream, which is flowing at one rate, and enter another timestream that is flowing at a slower rate. This is basically the opposite of taking a shortcut: taking a longcut. It's less

effort, but you need a sense of "when" you are and the rate the comparative stream flows. You step over, walk for a ways, and then step back.

These methods require you to have a sense of time and its layers, and some ability to manipulate it. Not everyone can, but that's okay—there are some other options later.

Contracting Time

Contracting time is essentially the opposite of expanding time. As the saying goes, "Time flies when you're having fun!" In this case, you want time to fly when you're not having fun, or when you need to be somewhere sooner than ordinary methods will allow.

Much the same concepts apply here as for expanding time. Decide whether you want to affect only yourself, or a small area including other people. Most folks who do temporal magic can handle a car-sized area, which is very useful! If you're contracting time to shorten a trip like that, it helps to put your hands on the vehicle when you cast the bubble; if you find that iron and plastics interfere with your magic, cast it big enough that the car won't touch the bubble edge.

There are multiple ways to work this trick too. If you're contracting time itself, pull from the inside, don't push from the outside. If you push, it will push back; you want to make it shrink inwards on itself with you at the center. Alternatively, you can take a shortcut. Step aside into a timestream that is flowing faster, which will carry you through the area sooner, and then step back into the consensus timestream.

Bending Time

In addition to being stretched or shrunk, time can also be bent. The usual application of this is to bend time so that it goes around some-

thing. This has two main effects: First, it makes the object last longer than usual, because most of the entropy is also going around it rather than through it. Second, it makes the object harder to find or manipulate from the outside, because the normal flow of time tends to carry things around it rather than let them get right on top of it. So it's similar in some ways to slowing time, but it's also akin to being "outside of time" as discussed below in ritual context.

A related matter is Fey or Faerie nature. Faeries—and mortals touched by Fey magic—tend to be "slippery" with regard to time. It's as if the consensus space-time continuum just can't get a firm grip on them. Time is more fluid in Fey places (stone circles, tree rings, etc.) or around Fey people. But it's not necessarily altered in the same

way every time—it may seem to run faster or slower, or have other odd effects, and then do something totally different on another occasion. If you know of places that have this effect, you can use their ability to influence timeflow, even if you don't have any of your own. So pay attention when you notice odd things happening with time.

Exiting and Entering Time

Pagan rituals typically happen "in a time that is not a time, in a place that is not a place." This is a good way to reduce the chance of interlopers stumbling across your ceremony. It creates a more mystical and spiritual atmosphere. It also facilitates the focusing of energy for various purposes. Departing from and returning to ordinary time are functions of casting the circle.

However, this works a bit differently than direct time manipulation, because it's more a side effect of creating sacred space. The gods and the world do the work. So you don't need an affinity for temporal magic per se, just a broader—and more common—ability to manipulate energy and consecrate the area.

The drawback is that you aren't in control of the timeflow, so you don't know exactly what's going to happen. Some rituals seem to take a long time, but after you release the circle only a few minutes have passed in consensus reality. Other rituals seem to take a reasonable amount of time, while hours and hours have passed on the clock. If you have a strong enough time-sense, you may be able to get an idea of what's going on in the consensus timestream. It's a good idea to make the best time estimate you can regarding how long your ritual will last ... and make sure you've got some leeway in case time does something odd.

Balancing Time

The space-time continuum contains certain features to relieve any imbalances. This helps keep the system stable overall. The most noticeable of these are locations that balance your personal time account when you cross them. If you tend to speed time, it will slow; if you tend to slow time, it will speed. There are also time sinks that consistently slow time or, more rarely, speed it. These usually appear on passageways such as roads or trails, where people will cross them frequently. Even ordinary people who rarely notice mystical things can spot these. It's another way to take advantage of time shifting if you don't have a particular talent for it, as long as you know where the relevant spots are.

Finally, remember that clocks and watches are anchors for the consensus timestream. They are strong but not invulnerable. If you're altering time, don't look at a clock, because it will tend to snap you back into objective time. Preferably, leave your timepieces out of the alteration zone, because odd things can happen. If you're wearing a watch when you shift time, it's likely to get out of phase with others; the same can happen to a clock that's in a room where you're altering time. If you alter time frequently, or if you're inherently slippery, any watch you wear may become unreliable after a while. So can a clock in a ritual room.

As long as you pay attention, you should be able to find ways of shifting time in your favor. Learn what your talents are and where you can take advantage of local time sinks. Used judiciously, this is a subtle magic that can be worked with no one the wiser.

Resources

Braschler, Von. "Perfect Timing: Mastering Time Perception for Performance Excellence." The Llewellyn Journal. www.llewellyn.com/journal/article/376 (accessed July 13, 2010).

Ellwood, Taylor. *Space/Time Magic*. Stafford, UK: Immanion Press/ Megalithica Books, 2005. Discussion of temporal magic and how to make it work for you.

Faige, David. "The Space-Time Continuum: A Thesis." Dave's Web Site. www.west.net/~ke6qp/spacetime/spacetime.html (accessed July 13, 2010).

Weinstock, John. "What Goes Around Comes Around: Sámi Time and Indigeneity." University of Texas. www.utexas.edu/courses/sami/dieda/anthro/time.htm (accessed July 13, 2010).

Candle Magic
by James Kambos

Somewhere tonight in a tiny apartment, a young lady lights the candles on a dinner table, completing the scene for a romantic dinner for two. And, at a kitchen table across town, a family gathers to watch a young boy as he makes a wish before blowing out the candles on his birthday cake.

Many people may not realize it, but what is actually taking place in these two scenes are examples of one of the world's most ancient forms of magic—candle magic.

Candle magic has been a part of folk magic, witchcraft and other religious ceremonies for centuries. A candle's flame has always been believed to attract benevolent spirits and to repel evil. Thus, candle magic in various forms has become woven into many religious and cultural rituals. Lighting candles in church or during Hanukkah are based on candle magic. The candles on a birthday cake are a hidden form of candle magic. It was believed that lighting candles on a birthday cake was a way to thank the Gods for prosperity and another year of life.

It is unknown when candle magic began, but we do know that candles have been a source of illumination in Crete and Egypt since about 3000 BCE.

Why and How Candle Magic Works

We've all experienced why candle magic works—candlelight is magical. You can easily transform an ordinary room into a place of mystery

and beauty simply by lighting a candle. Soft candlelight not only transforms a room into an enchanting space, it also transforms you, the magician. Candlelight raises our psychic awareness and prepares us for the magic to begin. It helps us forget about the mundane and allows us to focus on our magical goal.

The reason candle magic works is because of energy. When a candle is lit, it releases energy. And since you'll be the person who'll empower the candle, it will be *your* energy being released into the Unseen Realm.

Getting Started

Candle magic can be performed by just lighting a candle and saying a prayer. To receive more consistent results safely and easily however, here are some basic guidelines.

First, candle magic is used to bring a positive change into your life. In many magical rituals a candle is only a prop, used to enhance the magical process. But, in candle magic the candle *is* the magical tool, used to channel your power.

It also helps if you know the different parts associated with the candle and what their magical symbolism is. Most magicians agree the parts of a candle mirror the human body and spirit. I've found that a candle and the sections associated with it can be divided into six parts. I've listed them here, starting from the bottom to the top.

Holder: The holder or base represents Earth; the physical world. Eventually this is where your wish will manifest itself.

Wax: The wax is not only the body of the candle, it also symbolizes the human body. This is where you can personalize the candle by carving shapes or words into it. Later I'll explain in more detail how this section can be energized by your touch.

Wick: Unlit, the wick represents your potential. And when lit, the wick enables your wish to be released into the spirit realm.

Flame: During a candle ritual the flame naturally takes center stage. It symbolizes the Divine Spirit, and it will "talk" to you by sparking or moving in different directions. By watching the flame you can tell how a spell is working. If you're working with elementals such as salamanders, this is where you'll find them. It is also associated with entities such as the djinn (genies), since they were created from pure flame.

Halo: The glow or halo surrounding the flame is associated with the human aura. The halo is a good place to focus your attention during a scrying session.

Smoke: And finally there is smoke. Smoke serves as the messenger during candle magic. It carries your desire to the heavens. Depending the direction it drifts toward, it can also give you a clue how the wish will come to you.

The type of candle you use during a candle ritual is up to you. Candles made into human and animal shapes are sold at many occult shops, but can be expensive. Using simple taper, column, or votive candles is fine. So are scented candles which may help you achieve your magical goal.

Selecting a Candle Color

The color of the candle you use can make a difference. When in doubt, use white; I frequently do. Here is a list of colors and their magical associations.

Black: This is a color of mystery, not evil. Black can help get rid of negativity, or absorb unwanted energy and release it harmlessly.

Blue: The darker shades are good for growth and energy spells. The lighter shades bring peace and calm, and also soothe anger. Use blue to repel the evil eye.

Brown: Use brown to connect with Earth energy, trees, and gardens. It will also draw basic needs to you and promote stability.

Gold: This will attract energy, health, and power. Burning a gold candle will draw money to you which is owed to you.

Gray: Gray neutralizes negativity and removes it by making it inactive. It dispenses it harmlessly without karmic backlash. It's also good to use when you need to keep something secret.

Green: A healing color, green will aid in gardening, communicating with the fairy realm, and growth. But it will attract money to you only in small amounts.

Orange: A balance of red and yellow, an orange candle will draw money, energy, and vigorous health.

Pink: Not fiery like red, use pink for love and friendship. This is also a good color to calm emotions.

Purple: The royal color, purple will bring wealth, power, and

honor. This is also a good color to repel slander.

Red: Associated with Mars, red attracts lust and courage, and aids in protection. Use lighter reds only, darker shades can draw brute force.

White: The color of protection represents the Divine Spirit in its purest form. A safe bet if you're unsure of which color to use.

Yellow: Use yellow to relieve depression and to attract positive energy. It helps you retain knowledge and aids in communication.

Preparing a Candle for Ritual

To ensure that each spell is successful I urge you to take a few moments to prepare or "charge" your candle before a ritual. Here are a few tips.

You may begin by personalizing a candle by carving names, words, or symbols into the wax. These could be, but aren't limited to, runes, zodiac signs, a name, or a word such as "love."

As mentioned earlier, a candle is energized by your touch. This is sometimes called "dressing" the candle. To do this, hold your candle with both hands. With your right hand rub the candle from the center toward the wick. Release. Repeat with your left hand, moving from the center to the bottom of the candle, and release. Feel the energy building within the candle. Fragrant oils appropriate to your magical goal may also be used to dress the candle, or simply use olive oil. Rubbing the candle with herbs can give similar results.

Your candle is ready to use.

A Basic Candle Ritual

This ritual may be used for any wish; these are the basic steps for most candle magic spells.

Select a candle in the color you feel best represents your desire. Energize the candle by dressing it as described earlier. Concentrate and visualize your wish being answered. Using oils or herbs are optional. If you wish you may personalize the candle now by carving words or symbols into the wax. Place the candle into a secure holder.

You may perform some sympathetic magic by placing photographs, keys, or any other personal items around the holder. Be sure they're protected from the flame and melting wax.

Now, ground and center. Light the candle. Your magic has begun. Watch the flame closely. If it burns steady your wish is coming soon. A sparking, crackling type of flame points to obstacles or arguments. If the flame returns to a steady burn, your desire will eventually come to fruition. A flame that gutters out means you're facing many obstacles, and you should try your spell another day.

If the smoke wafts over you, your request is being heard by the Divine.

To end a session, snuff out the flame, never blow it out. And never leave a candle burning unattended. Don't reuse a candle, unless you're going to work on the same spell over several days.

Above all, look and listen to the flame and smoke. Eventually, you'll begin to understand their language as you master this ancient form of fire magic.

Scrapbooking Your BOS
by Tabitha Bradley

For most Witches, one of the first things you do when you begin to pratice the Craft is start your own Book of Shadows. Whether it is a simple, spiral-bound notebook or a bound journal, your first BOS is an important part of your growth and development.

Most of us have seen Books of Shadows we'd love to have: those thick, ancient tomes of wonderful knowledge that look as though they contain the very secrets of the universe. Who can forget the gorgeous books from the TV show *Charmed* and the movie *Practical Magic*? Of course, those are designed by prop departments and are entirely fictional, but I've seen some pretty impressive real-life Books that only served to intimidate the heck out of me.

I'm not much for bound journals (I never seem to want to write in them; being an author, I'm always wanting to change things), and somehow a plain old notebook wasn't special enough. So I went the middle way most of us busy Witchy moms do and I got a three-ring binder, a paper hole punch, and some plastic page protectors. What I didn't have page protectors for, I printed and punched holes in. Needless to say, my Book was pretty boring looking. Well, I *did* use some colored copier paper from time to time.

Then my mom introduced me to scrapbooking. I've never been much for keeping my photo albums up to date, so even though it looked like so much fun, I figured it wasn't going to work for my pictures. However, what I did see when I entered my first scrapbooking shop was an awful lot of cool stuff to make my BOS less boring—particularly the patterned papers and albums that looked like bound books. Of course, the stickers, ribbons, sparkly inks, and stamps certainly helped as well.

So what occurred to me was that here was a way to make a plain BOS fun and unique while still creating a document could be passed down through the family. A major point of scrapbooking is preservation, so when you're getting supplies from scrapbook shops, you're nearly guaranteed to find things that are made to last and preserve the effort you're putting into your pages, which is exactly what we want when making a family or coven BOS.

Other folks have figured this out as well, so now there are even specific embellishments and other supplies created specifically for scrapbooking your Book of Shadows. I've included some of those resources at the end of this article.

I recommend you start with a three-ring binder, which makes it easy to change around and remove pages as you go. You can also do this with specially designed scrapbooking albums, but the pages tend to be harder to rearrange since these are built like photo albums. Albums can be a more permanent solution once you have figured out your preferred arrangement. Specialty albums are also more expensive than your standard three-ring binder and are more commonly available in larger sizes than standard letter size. It is becoming more common to find albums designed for digital scrapbooking now, which use the more common paper sizes. This is a nice alternative if you'd like something that looks a bit more like a book, rather than an office binder. I've tried both methods and prefer beginning with the binder. This also gives you more money to spend on embellishments and paper.

Once you have your binder, you'll need plastic page protectors. These are necessary if you plan to use 3D elements like clips, buttons, ribbons, brads—anything that will rise off the surface of the paper. The page protectors keep your embellishments from getting damaged by the rest of the contents of the book, as well as keep decorations in position. There are methods for making page protectors work with advanced techniques like double-page layouts and interactive elements, but those are a bit complex for our beginner Scrapbook of Shadows.

Along with the binder and page protectors, you'll need paper. It's best to start with card stock paper, which is thick enough to support your decorations. (Paper is graded in weights: card stock begins at 60 lbs. while regular paper is 20 to 25 lbs.)

If you decide to get some decorative paper as well, 20 lb. paper is fine. There is a wide variety of decorative paper from which to choose—you will also find different kinds of papers, like parchment, mulberry paper, and even papyrus in some stores. All of this can be used subtly or to make aspects of the page jump out. You can print or write a poem on decorative paper and layer it on your background page with a slip of contrasting mulberry paper in between for a lovely effect.

The rest of your supplies will be relatively simple. If you're going to handwrite in your book, invest in a good set of acid-free pens in standard colors. You may need a 3-hole punch if you choose not to use page protectors. A glue stick is another must—particularly when using semi-transparent papers like mulberry. Glue sticks are less messy and dry more quickly than liquid glues. (An acid-free glue stick will also help preserve your pages.) If you choose to use larger and heavier elements, you will need glue dots, which are designed for this purpose. You will need regular paper scissors and a craft knife for detail work. The last tool you need to get will be a paper cutter. These range from the big office cutters to simple sliding cutters that you can find in any scrapbooking and craft department. (Make sure the sliding crafts cutter is at least 11.5 inches long and can handle the largest paper you're using.)

From here on you will be selecting decorative elements based on what your page will be about. I would not recommend just going to the scrapbook or crafts section of your local shop and just buying whatever

looks cool or pretty! That adds up fast and you end up with a lot of elements you may or may not be able to use in the long run. Even "starter packs" of embellishments can be hit or miss (although starter packs of paper is a good idea as long as you stick to the basics).

I'd start simple and plan one page at a time. For instance, if you're going to do holidays, pick a sabbat and think of the colors you want to use. Start with your foundation paper in a basic color and build the page from there. If you're going to use written information, decide whether you're going to handwrite it or print it from your computer, and plan accordingly. Handwritten information will tend to take up more space, so you may end up needing more than one page. Then you can add whatever decorations you like. Stickers, little

3D decorations, frames, and ribbons all dress up a page and are fun to collect, particularly in themes like holidays and special occasions.

You may find yourself creating more pages on a subject than you would in a simple printed Book of Shadows, since scrapbooking encourages journaling and sharing memories. You may decide to include a ritual for a holiday on one page, another page decorated with recipes, and another with pictures from your last celebration of that sabbat. Scrapbooking brings out creativity you may not have realized you had.

There are plenty of resources out there: magazines, books, Internet sites, and podcasts that will help you learn more about this exciting and fun hobby. They will teach you various methods and styles of scrapbooking, such as digital, vintage, and shabby chic; show you different styles of laying out pages; and introduce you to other scrappers around the world, including *other* Wiccans scrapping their Books of Shadows!

I hope I've given you enough information to get started on creating your own totally unique Book of Shadows. Here are some sites you can visit to generate ideas and kick-start the scrapbooking process.

Pagan-Themed Scrapbooking Supplies

Book of Shadows 3-Ring Binders: www.zazzle.com/frootbat31

Pagan Scrapbooking Embellishments: www.thepointyhat.com/Pagan-Scrapbooking_c_68.html

Magick Stamp Kit by Ann Kay: Available at online retailers.

Online Scrapbook and Craft Stores: www.scrapbooking-warehouse.com, www.scrapbook.com, www.twopeasinabucket.com

Free Printables: www.scrapbookscrapbook.com

Digital Scrapbooking: www.renderosity.com (Marketplace under "2-D/scrapbooking"), www.digitalscrapbookplace.com, shabbyprincess.com, www.scrapbookgraphics.com

December/January

26 Monday

1st ♑
☽ v/c 8:36 am
☽ enters ♒ 12:14 pm
Color: Lavender

For optimism and gentle encouragement, use the color peach

27 Tuesday

1st ♒
Color: Red

28 Wednesday

4th ♒
☽ v/c 4:31 pm
☽ enters ♓ 6:45 pm
Color: Brown

Turtle is a totem for children in general;
it conveys patience, protection, and longevity

29 Thursday

1st ♓
Color: Purple

The Golden Rectangle symbolizes idealism
and the meeting of humanity and divinity

30 Friday

1st ♓
☽ v/c 8:37 am
Color: White

31 Saturday

1st ♓
☽ enters ♈ 4:48 am
Color: Gray

New Year's Eve

◖ Sunday

1st ♈
2nd quarter 1:15 am
Color: Gold

New Year's Day
Kwanzaa ends
Birthday of Sir James Frazer,
author of *The Golden Bough*, 1854

January

2 Monday
2nd ♈
☽ v/c 3:07 pm
☽ enters ♉ 5:16 pm
Color: Ivory

*Yerba santa incense is called "the
portable temple" because it cleanses and
consecrates the area where it is burned*

3 Tuesday
2nd ♉
Color: Scarlet

Death of Edgar Cayce, psychic, 1945

4 Wednesday
2nd ♉
Color: Topaz

Aquarian Tabernacle Church
registered in Australia by
Lady Tamara Von Forslun, 1994

5 Thursday
2nd ♉
☽ v/c 3:46 am
☽ enters ♊ 5:44 am
Color: Crimson

6 Friday
2nd ♊
Color: Purple

Twelfth Night/Epiphany

Patricia Crowther's witchcraft
radio show, *A Spell of Witchcraft*,
airs in Britain, 1971

Set in Eastern Standard Time (EST)

Peace and Quiet

To recover from the holiday rush, use calming lavender and a white or blue candle. If possible, do this spell in a quiet, darkened room. Dab the oil on the candle and breathe slowly and deeply. After saying the spell, sit and enjoy the peace for a while.

> *Stillness and shadow, silence and*
> *   peace*
> *Banish the hurry, let time itself cease*
> *Cloak me in quiet, calming my soul*
> *Mending the pieces, leaving me whole*
> *Let cares fall away like the autumn leaf's flurry*
> *Blow away trouble, wash away worry*
> *Leave peace like a blanket, snuggly and warm*
> *Safe from all fear, safe from all harm*
> *The quiet of winter, in darkness I find*
> *A peace of the soul to quiet my mind*
> *Let me relax and find my own center*
> *As into the silence I happily enter*
> —Deborah Blake

---

7 Saturday

2nd ♊
☽ v/c 2:52 pm
☽ enters ♋ 4:05 pm
Color: Blue

---

8 Sunday

2nd ♋
☿ enters ♑ 1:34 am
Color: Amber

Birthday of MacGregor Mathers,
one of the three original founders
of the Golden Dawn, 1854
Death of Dion Fortune, 1946

January

☺ Monday

2nd ♋
Full Moon 2:30 am
☽ v/c 9:25 pm
☽ enters ♌ 11:35 pm
Color: Lavender

Cold Moon

Jamie Dodge wins lawsuit against
the Salvation Army, which fired her
based on her Wiccan religion, 1989

10 Tuesday

3rd ♌
Color: Red

For support when dealing with issues of guilt, use pine wood

11 Wednesday

3rd ♌
Color: Yellow

12 Thursday

3rd ♌
☽ v/c 3:23 am
☽ enters ♍ 4:44 am
Color: Green

Mary Smith hanged in England;
she had quarreled with neighbors,
who said that the Devil appeared
to her as a black man, 1616

13 Friday

3rd ♍
☽ v/c 8:58 pm
Color: Rose

Final witchcraft laws
repealed in Austria, 1787

Set in Eastern Standard Time (EST)

The Comforting Crab Moon

The energy of this Full Moon is embodied by the Crab. A creature of land and sea, Crab evokes the complex emotions involved in that most basic support system: one's home and family. While Crabs can be aggressive toward each other, they also work together to feed and protect their families. Crab teaches us the importance of protecting one's sense of self while maintaining the integrity of the home and family.

On this Cancer Full Moon, follow your Crab Within into a safe space for reflection and comfort. Today, as the energies of earth and water combine at the height of Moon's power, prepare a healing bath for yourself. While the warm water is filling the tub, mix 4 tablespoons of sea salt, 2 tablespoons of olive oil, and 1 tablespoon of lemon juice. Consider a challenge to the harmony in your home or your family. Reflect on the sources of this challenge and its manifestations as you scrub the salt mixture over your body. Feel the salt draw the toxins from you as it rejuvenates body, mind, and spirit. As the water cleanses the salt from your body, visualize healing flowing into this situation and ask for guidance on how you might contribute to that healing.

—Kristin Madden

14 Saturday

3rd ♍
♀ enters ♓ 12:47 am
☽ enters ♎ 8:28 am
Color: Black

Official Confession of Error by jurors of Salem Witch Trials, 1696
Human Be-In, a Pagan-style festival, takes place in San Francisco, attended by Timothy Leary and Allen Ginsburg, 1967

15 Sunday

3rd ♎
Color: Yellow

◑ Monday

3rd ♎
4th quarter 4:08 am
☽ v/c 10:29 am
☽ enters ♏ 11:33 am
Color: Silver

Birthday of Martin Luther King, Jr. (observed)
Birthday of Dr. Dennis Carpenter, Circle Sanctuary

17 Tuesday

4th ♏
Color: Black

Indigo inspires idealism, wisdom, and justice

18 Wednesday

4th ♏
☽ v/c 1:31 pm
☽ enters ♐ 2:29 pm
Color: Brown

19 Thursday

4th ♐
♃ enters ♈ 1:37 pm
Color: White

Birthday of Dorothy Clutterbuck,
who initiated Gerald Gardner, 1880

20 Friday

4th ♐
☉ enters ♒ 11:10 am
☽ v/c 4:49 pm
☽ enters ♑ 5:40 pm
Color: Pink

Sun enters Aquarius

Guidance and Direction

To ask for direction in the year to come, use a yellow candle; if desired, use a sprig of rosemary to stir a bowl of water—then look within the bowl for answers. Or you can dab some rosemary essential oil on the candle.

> I ask for guidance in this new year
> To take me where I'm meant to be
> A path to walk, a voice to hear
> A signpost through life's mystery
> Send direction for my journey
> And inspiration for my heart
> Lay my passage clear before me
> So I might make a proper start

Afterward, be sure to keep your eyes open for signs that might indicate that the universe is sending you the guidance you asked for!

—Deborah Blake

21 Saturday
4th ♑
Color: Blue

Celtic Tree Month of Rowan begins

22 Sunday
4th ♑
☽ v/c 8:38 pm
☽ enters ♒ 9:53 pm
Color: Orange

January

☽ Monday
4th ≈
New Moon 2:39 am
♂ ℞ 7:54 pm
Color: Gray

Chinese New Year (dragon)

24 Tuesday
1st ≈
Color: Red

*The Chinese goddess Ma Zhu watches
over travel, journeys, and wayfarers*

25 Wednesday

1st ≈
☽ v/c 3:33 am
☽ enters ♓ 4:11 am
Color: Topaz

Birthday of Robert Burns, Scottish poet, 1759

26 Thursday

1st ♓
☽ v/c 11:53 pm
Color: Green

27 Friday
1st ♓
☿ enters ≈ 1:12 pm
☽ enters ♈ 1:28 pm
Color: Coral

*Dawn is a good time to cast 24-hour spells;
many temporary forms of magic are broken by dawn*

Set in Eastern Standard Time (EST)

Brigid's Blessing Salad

4 cups baby spinach leaves
1 cup edible seed sprouts (sunflower
  or pea sprouts, spicy radish, etc.)
16 jumbo shrimp
1 cup fresh mango, cubed
2 T. fresh ginger root, finely diced
Sunflower seeds, pumpkin seeds
A pinch of cilantro

Vinaigrette
2 T. Dijon mustard
2 T. mayonnaise
2 T. honey
Dash of lemon juice
¼ cup balsamic vinegar

In a nonstick frying pan on medium heat, gently sauté ginger. When it turns opaque, add shrimp and sauté until they turn pink. Do not overcook. Turn heat to high, add mango chunks, saute for 1 minute. Serve on beds of baby spinach, and top with sprouts and seeds. Shake all vinaigrette ingredients together in a jar, then drizzle over salad, and top with a pinch of cilantro. A visually gorgeous salad with contrasting colors and textures.

—Dallas Jennifer Cobb

28 Saturday
1st ♈
Color: Brown

Use willow wood to work with cycles and rhythms

29 Sunday
1st ♈
⚵ enters ♐ 9:13 am
Color: Yellow

January/February

○ Monday

1st ♈
☽ v/c 1:08 am
☽ enters ♉ 1:28 am
2nd quarter 11:10 pm
Color: White

Birthday of Zsuzsanna E. Budapest, feminist Witch

31 Tuesday

2nd ♉
Color: White

Dr. Fian, believed to be the head
of the North Berwick Witches, found
guilty and executed for witchcraft in
Scotland by personal order of King
James VI (James I of England), 1591

1 Wednesday

2nd ♉
☽ v/c 2:06 pm
☽ enters ♊ 2:14 pm
Color: White

2 Thursday

2nd ♊
Color: Turquoise

Imbolc
Groundhog Day
Leo Martello becomes a third-degree
Welsh traditionalist, 1973

3 Friday

2nd ♊
♆ enters ♓ 2:03 pm
Color: Pink

For greater awareness of cause and effect, use kyanite

Set in Eastern Standard Time (EST)

Imbolc

Snow is on the ground, and the cold grip of winter seems as though it will never give way. However, on Imbolc, spring is not as far away as it seems. At this time, we call upon the goddess Bridget to warm, heal, and inspire us. As a Celtic Triple Goddess of healing, smithcraft, and poetry, Bridget's powers are many, and they are never far away.

Bridget can help bring the healing powers of sacred herbs into our mind, body, and spirit during these difficult weeks of winter. As a goddess of smithcraft and mistress of the elements, she reminds us to use the power of the elements to balance, ground, and rejuvenate ourselves. And as a goddess of poetry, we can call on her to summon the warm flame of inspiration.

In Ireland and Scotland, groups of women carried a corn dolly Bridget from home to home. She was presented to those within, who honored her and decorated "Bridget's Bed" with flowers, shells, stones, and ribbons. Make a likeness of Bridget and light a sacred flame to honor her, intoning these hallowed words from traditional Irish Imbolc rituals held at home: "Bridget is here, Bridget is welcome, Bridget is here, Bridget is welcome."

—Sharynne MacLeod NicMhacha

4 Saturday

2nd ♊
☽ v/c 12:06 am
☽ enters ♋ 1:04 am
Color: Black

Imbolc crossquarter day
(Sun reaches 15° Aquarius)

5 Sunday

2nd ♋
Color: Orange

February

6 Monday

2nd ♋
☽ v/c 7:31 am
☽ enters ♌ 8:24 am
Color: Ivory

☺ Tuesday

2nd ♌
♄ ℞ 9:03 am
Full Moon 4:54 pm
Color: Maroon

Quickening Moon

Death of Thomas Aquinas, scholar who
wrote that heresy was a product of
ignorance and therefore criminal, and
who refuted the *Canon Episcopi*, 1274

8 Wednesday

3rd ♌
♀ enters ♈ 1:01 am
☽ v/c 11:42 am
☽ enters ♍ 12:32 pm
Color: Brown

Birthday of Susun Weed, owner of
Wise Woman Publishing

Birthday of Evangeline Adams,
American astrologer, 1868

9 Thursday

3rd ♍
Color: Purple

10 Friday

3rd ♍
☽ v/c 12:11 am
☽ enters ♎ 2:54 pm
Color: Rose

Zsuzsanna Budapest arrested and later
convicted for fortunetelling, 1975

Set in Eastern Standard Time (EST)

The Powerful Lion Moon

The "King of the Beasts," the lion has been worshipped for thousands of years as a symbol of power, strength, and royalty. The teachings of Buddha are also known as the "Lion's Roar" for their strength and power. Very few creatures will challenge a lion—even humans are cautious. Lions have much to teach us about maintaining strong bonds of family and community while holding our own power in healthy ways. We are

reminded that we can be gentle and play without giving up strength. The lion shines through the Leo Full Moon, filling our lives with this energy.

Reclaim your power and embody your strength at this Full Moon. Don't howl at the Moon—roar! Consider if you identify more with the African lion or the cougar of the Americas. Put on some drumming or music that evokes the cultures that evolved with that animal. Sit and feel your physical strength and your sensuality. Move to the music like a lion. As you stretch and stalk, consider how you hold your power, how you have given some up, and how you go after what you want. Ask the Lion Within how to reclaim your power and hunt success in the most honorable and regal ways possible.

—Kristin Madden

11 Saturday

3rd ♎
Color: Blue

Teaching both patience and decisive action, cougar is an apt totem for people in dangerous professions

12 Sunday

3rd ♎
♀ enters ♓ 12:05 am
☽ v/c 4:09 pm
☽ enters ♏ 5:01 pm
Color: Gold

Gerald Gardner, founder of the Gardnerian tradition, dies of heart failure, 1964

February

13 Monday
3rd ♏
☿ enters ♓ 8:38 pm
Color: Silver

Burn orange to attract love and luck

◐ Tuesday
3rd ♏
☽ v/c 12:04 pm
4th quarter 12:04 pm
☽ enters ♐ 7:56 pm
Color: Gray

Valentine's Day
Elsie Blum, a farmhand from
Oberstedten, Germany, sentenced
to death for witchcraft, 1652

15 Wednesday
4th ♐
Color: Brown

Pope Leo X issues papal bull to ensure that
the secular courts carry out executions
of Witches convicted by the Inquisition,
1521; the bull was a response to the courts'
refusal to carry out the work of the Church

16 Thursday
4th ♐
☽ v/c 11:03 pm
Color: Green

17 Friday
4th ♐
☽ enters ♑ 12:03 am
Color: White

Encourage a broken heart to heal with a violet leaf

18 Saturday

4th ♑
Color: Gray

Celtic Tree Month of Ash begins

19 Sunday

4th ♑
☉ enters ♓ 1:18 am
☽ v/c 4:22 am
☽ enters ♒ 5:28 am
Color: Orange

Sun enters Pisces

Set in Eastern Standard Time (EST)   43

February

20 Monday

4th ≈
Color: Lavender

Presidents' Day (observed)

🌙 Tuesday

4th ≈
☽ v/c 11:17 am
☽ enters ♓ 12:31 pm
New Moon 5:35 pm
Color: Red

Mardi Gras (Fat Tuesday)
Birthday of Patricia Telesco, Wiccan author
Stewart Farrar initiated into Alexandrian Wicca, 1970
Death of Theodore Parker Mills, 1996

22 Wednesday

1st ♓
☽ v/c 9:24 pm
Color: Yellow

Ash Wednesday
Birthday of Sybil Leek, Wiccan author, 1922

23 Thursday

1st ♓
☽ enters ♈ 9:48 pm
Color: Purple

The infinity sign represents that which is cyclic yet unchanging

24 Friday
1st ♈
Color: White

Set in Eastern Standard Time (EST)

Planting Seeds

To plant the seeds for those things you wish to flourish in the days ahead, write down what you want to grow, and then light a green candle. If you want, place some seeds (pumpkin, sunflower, etc.) into a bowl, and eat them after saying the spell. Put the list on your altar to remind you of what you are working toward!

> *Deep the earth below my feet*
> *Dark the ground and dark the night*
> *Turn the wheel of the year*
> *Bringing life and bringing light*
> *I plant the seeds for what I want*
> *For all I need and all I seek*
> *Vowing now to do the work*
> *Planting magick as I speak*
> —Deborah Blake

25 Saturday

1st ♈
♆ enters ♈ 2:05 pm
Color: Indigo

26 Sunday

1st ♈
☽ v/c 7:52 am
☽ enters ♉ 9:29 am
Color: Amber

For restful sleep, point the head of the bed north

February/March

27 Monday

1st ♉
Color: Gray

Pope John XXII issues first papal bull to
discuss the practice of witchcraft, 1318

Birthday of Rudolf Steiner, philosopher and
father of the biodynamic farming movement, 1861

28 Tuesday

1st ♉
☽ v/c 2:46 pm
☽ enters ♊ 10:27 pm
Color: Black

*A time change creates a "break" in the
flow of time when you can make things
disappear, or re-envision the past*

◐ Wednesday

1st ♊
2nd quarter 8:21 pm
Color: Topaz

Leap Day

1 Thursday

2nd ♊
Color: Turquoise

Preliminary hearings in the
Salem Witch trials held, 1692

Birthday of the Golden Dawn, 1888

Covenant of the Goddess (COG) formed, 1975

2 Friday

2nd ♊
☿ enters ♈ 6:41 am
☽ v/c 8:14 am
☽ enters ♋ 10:08 am
Color: Rose

Set in Eastern Standard Time (EST)

3 Saturday
2nd ♋
Color: Blue

4 Sunday
2nd ♋
☽ v/c 5:17 pm
☽ enters ♌ 6:17 pm
Color: Yellow

Church of All Worlds incorporates in
Missouri, 1968, becoming the first Pagan
church to incorporate in the United States

March

5 Monday

2nd ♌
♀ enters ♉ 5:25 am
Color: Lavender

Leopardskin jasper stabilizes chakras and eases frustrations

6 Tuesday

2nd ♌
☽ v/c 8:27 pm
☽ enters ♍ 10:27 pm
Color: Scarlet

Birthday of Laurie Cabot, Wiccan author

7 Wednesday

2nd ♍
Color: Yellow

William Butler Yeats initiated
into the Isis-Urania Temple
of the Golden Dawn, 1890

☺ Thursday

2nd ♍
☽ v/c 4:39 am
Full Moon 4:39 am
☽ enters ♎ 11:50 pm
Color: Green

Purim
Storm Moon

9 Friday

3rd ♎
Color: Pink

Turquoise supports fellowship and community

Set in Eastern Standard Time (EST)

The Community Ant Moon

The Virgo Full Moon brings through the energy of practicality and the need for order in society. This energy is epitomized by Ant energy. These creatures have amazingly complex societies. Each ant has its job and lives to do the best job it can do for the community. Humans value individuality, but we can lose sight of community in our struggle to be unique and important.

On one hand, Ant asks if we are turning our backs on our communities as we look out for "Number One." On the other hand, Ant may warn you that you have lost sight of your own individuality. This is an ideal time to explore these choices in a very practical way. As an individual or with a community, such as a grove or coven, make three lists. One list records all the ways you feel both empowered as an individual and of service to your community. The other list includes ways you feel devalued, overworked, or put on a pedestal above other community members. Brainstorm ways to bring balance to the situations described by list 2. Once you feel you have a useful third list, burn list 2 and bury the ashes in the earth. Ask the Great Mother to help you find a more balanced way of being in community.

—Kristin Madden

10 Saturday

3rd ♎
☽ v/c 10:09 pm
Color: Black

Date recorded for first meeting of
Dr. John Dee and Edward Kelley, 1582
Dutch clairvoyant and psychic
healer Gerard Croiser born, 1909

11 Sunday

3rd ♎
☽ enters ♏ 12:24 am
Color: Amber

Daylight Saving Time begins at 2 am

March

12 Monday

3rd ♏
☿ Ɽ 3:49 am
☽ v/c 2:30 pm
Color: White

Stewart Edward White, psychic
researcher, born, 1873; he later
became president of the
American Society for Psychical
Research in San Francisco

13 Tuesday

3rd ♏
☽ enters ♐ 2:54 am
Color: Gray

Yew wood assists in seeking visions

☽ Wednesday

3rd ♐
4th quarter 9:25 pm
Color: Topaz

15 Thursday

4th ♐
☽ v/c 3:34 am
☽ enters ♑ 6:24 am
Color: Crimson

Pete Pathfinder Davis becomes the first Wiccan
priest elected as president of the
Interfaith Council of Washington State, 1995

16 Friday

4th ♑
Color: Coral

Sandalwood incense furthers psychic development and the subtle senses

Eoster Eggs

Whole wheat bread,
    one slice per person
Egg, one per person
Butter, best at room temperature

Heat a nonstick frying pan to medium heat. Butter both sides of bread, then carefully cut an egg shaped opening in the middle of the bread, and remove the center. Place the bread in frying pan, with center piece off to the side, and fry. When one side is finished, carefully turn bread pieces over.

Crack the egg and pour it into the center opening of the main bread piece. This represents the union of sun and soil, the equality of God and Goddess. Cover, and cook until egg white is hardened, and yolk is creamy perfection. Remove from frying pan and place on a plate, carefully placing the toasted oval shape over the egg yolk. Garnish with fruit or flowers, and serve. As you dip your toast ovals into the rich egg yolk, or cut squares of egg-laden toast, know the power of the union of God and Goddess. Invoke fertility, prosperity, and potential in your life; celebrate new beginnings and feast on the fertile union of sun and soil.

—Dallas Jennifer Cobb

17 Saturday

4th ♑
☽ v/c 9:00 am
☽ enters ♒ 12:11 pm
Color: Blue

St. Patrick's Day
Eleanor Shaw and Mary Phillips
executed in England for bewitching a
woman and her two children, 1705

18 Sunday

4th ♒
Color: Gold

Celtic Tree Month of Alder begins
Birthday of Edgar Cayce, psychic researcher, 1877

March

19 Monday

4th ≈
☽ v/c 4:31 pm
☽ enters ♓ 8:05 pm
Color: Ivory

Elizabethan statute against witchcraft
enacted, 1563; this statute was replaced in
1604 by a stricter one from King James I

20 Tuesday

4th ♓
☉ enters ♈ 1:14 am
Color: White

Ostara/Spring Equinox
Sun enters Aries
International Astrology Day
Death of Lady Sheba, Wiccan author
of *The Book of Shadows*, 2002

21 Wednesday

4th ♓
☽ v/c 4:39 am
Color: Brown

Mandate of Henry VIII against witchcraft
enacted, 1542; repealed in 1547
Green Egg magazine founded, 1968

☽ Thursday

4th ♓
☽ enters ♈ 5:57 am
New Moon 10:37 am
Color: White

Pope Clement urged by Phillip IV
to suppress Templar Order, 1311

23 Friday

1st ♈
☿ enters ♓ 9:22 am
Color: Purple

Set in Eastern Daylight Time (EDT)

Spring Equinox

Spring Equinox is a sacred time of balance, growth, and rebirth. The hours of light and dark are equal, and although the early winds of spring still have a chill to them, signs of rebirth and renewal abound. The increase in sunlight tells us to come out of our dens and open ourselves to the stirrings of springtime's beauty.

Make a point to notice every sign of spring in the local landscape. Which birds have returned from their winter homes? What are the first flowers to appear? Welcome and honor each type of plant and flower that raises itself from the ground. Greet the plant spirits of snowdrop, crocus, and daffodil, or whatever native plants grow. Each plant contains healing and wisdom, if we take the time to listen.

Make a springtime altar near a doorway of your home, signifying balance of growth within and growth without. Decorate it with springtime flowers, colored eggs, and images of sacred animals—small birds, rabbits, and others you work with. Take a small container of soil and plant four seeds, one for each direction. Using your breath, blow your intentions for balance, growth, and transformation into each seed as you plant it in the earth.

—Sharynne MacLeod NicMhacha

---

24 Saturday

1st ♈
☽ v/c 1:17 pm
☽ enters ♉ 5:43 pm
☿ ℞ 7:32 pm
Color: Brown

Arrest of Florence Newton, one of the few Witches burned in Ireland, 1661

---

25 Sunday

1st ♉
Color: Orange

Pope Innocent III issues papal bull to establish the Inquisition, 1199

March/April

26 Monday
1st ♉
Color: Gray

Birthday of Joseph Campbell, author
and professor of mythology, 1910

27 Tuesday
1st ♉
☽ v/c 12:35 am
☽ enters ♊ 6:43 am
Color: Red

If you are super-sensitive,
carry Botswana agate as a buffer

28 Wednesday
1st ♊
Color: Yellow

Death of Scott Cunningham,
Wiccan author, 1993

29 Thursday
1st ♊
☽ v/c 2:05 pm
☽ enters ♋ 7:07 pm
Color: Green

☽ Friday
1st ♋
2nd quarter 3:41 pm
Color: White

Rattlesnake root protects against liars and false friends

Set in Eastern Daylight Time (EDT)

31 Saturday

2nd ♋
Color: Gray

Last Witch trial in Ireland,
held at Magee Island, 1711

1 Sunday

2nd ♋
☽ v/c 12:20 am
☽ enters ♌ 4:35 am
Color: Gold

Palm Sunday
April Fools' Day (All Fools' Day—Pagan)

April

2 Monday
2nd ♌
Color: Silver

Spells for growth and new projects get a boost from spring

3 Tuesday
2nd ♌
☽ v/c 9:47 am
☽ enters ♍ 9:53 am
♀ enters ♊ 11:18 am
Color: White

4 Wednesday
2nd ♍
☿ D 6:11 am
Color: White

5 Thursday
2nd ♍
☽ v/c 1:37 am
☽ enters ♎ 11:32 am
Color: Crimson

Trial of Alice Samuel, her husband, and her daughter, who were accused of bewitching the wife of Sir Henry Cromwell and several village children, 1593

☺ Friday
2nd ♎
Full Moon 3:19 pm
Color: Coral

Wind Moon
Good Friday

Set in Eastern Daylight Time (EDT)

The Peaceful Crane Moon

In Asia, it is said that folding 1,000 origami cranes will make your dreams come true. That's why a Japanese girl named Sadako tried to do so during her treatment for leukemia, a result of the bombing of Hiroshima. Sadako never finished, but people from all over the world fold cranes and send them to the Children's Monument at the Hiroshima Peace Park. The monument reads: "This is our cry. This is our prayer. Peace in the world."

On this Libra Full Moon, work for peace and harmony. Draw a rough outline of a crane in salt on a plate, pouring into the salt all your beliefs about finding inner peace or witnessing world peace. Allow the salt's bitterness to soak up your fears and doubts. Pour the salt into a bowl of water. As you watch those beliefs and emotions dissolve, recite the Druid's Peace Prayer:

> *Deep within the still center of my being, may I find peace.*
> *Silently within the quiet of the Grove, may I share peace.*
> *Gently and powerfully, within the greater circle of humankind,*
> *   may I radiate peace.*

—Kristin Madden

7 Saturday

3rd ♎
☽ v/c 6:15 am
☽ enters ♏ 11:18 am
Color: Black

Passover begins
Church of All Worlds founded, 1962
First Wiccan "tract" published
by Pete Pathfinder Davis, 1996

8 Sunday

3rd ♏
Color: Amber

Easter
William Alexander Aynton initiated into the
Isis-Urania Temple of the Golden
Dawn, 1896; he would later be called the
"Grand Old Man" of the Golden Dawn

April

9 Monday

3rd ♏
☽ v/c 2:56 am
☽ enters ♐ 11:12 am
♀ enters ♉ 4:39 pm
Color: Ivory

The Australian storm god Mamaragan lives in a
puddle when not throwing thunder and lightning

10 Tuesday

3rd ♐
♇ R 12:21 pm
Color: Maroon

Birthday of Rev. Montague Summers,
orthodox scholar and author of
A History of Witchcraft and Demonology, 1880

11 Wednesday

3rd ♐
☽ v/c 7:06 am
☽ enters ♑ 1:02 pm
Color: Brown

Burning of Major Weir, Scottish "sorcerer" who
confessed of his own accord, 1670; some histori-
ans believe that the major became delusional or
senile because up until his confession he had an
excellent reputation and was a pillar of society

12 Thursday

3rd ♑
Color: Purple

☽ Friday

3rd ♑
4th quarter 6:50 am
☽ v/c 1:05 pm
☽ enters ♒ 5:48 pm
♂ D 11:53 pm
Color: Pink

Orthodox Good Friday

Spring Cleaning

To cleanse and purify both body and spirit, light a white candle. Before saying the spell, use a bowl of water to symbolically wash your hands, or take a ritual bath with cleansing herbs (rosemary, mint, sage). Visualize the four elements cleansing you.

Goddess of the spring
Send your swift breezes
To cleanse my spirit
Send your laughing waters
To cleanse my mind
Send your bright fire
To cleanse my heart
And your pure earth
To cleanse my body
Let me be remade
Clean and new
In your image
So I might rise again
Like the phoenix in spring
                    —Deborah Blake

---

14 Saturday

4th ≈
Color: Indigo

Passover ends
Adoption of the Principles of
Wiccan Belief at "Witch Meet"
in St. Paul, Minnesota, 1974

---

15 Sunday

4th ≈
☽ v/c 6:42 pm
Color: Gold

Orthodox Easter
Celtic Tree Month of Willow begins
Birthday of Elizabeth Montgomery,
who played Samantha on *Bewitched*, 1933

April

16 Monday

4th ≈
☽ enters ♓ 1:38 am
☿ enters ♈ 6:42 pm
Color: Silver

Birthday of Margot Adler, author
of *Drawing Down the Moon*

17 Tuesday

4th ♓
☽ v/c 10:34 am
Color: Red

Aleister Crowley breaks into and takes over the
Golden Dawn temple, providing the catalyst for
the demise of the original Golden Dawn, 1900

18 Wednesday

4th ♓
☽ enters ♈ 11:59 am
Color: Yellow

19 Thursday

4th ♈
☉ enters ♉ 12:12 pm
Color: Green

Sun enters Taurus

Conviction of Witches
at second of four famous trials at
Chelmsford, England, 1579

20 Friday

4th ♈
☽ v/c 3:35 pm
Color: Pink

Set in Eastern Daylight Time (EDT)

Love in Bloom

To open your heart to love in all its positive forms, light a red or pink candle and visualize your heart chakra opening up and blooming like a flower. If you want, put a rose on your altar, or dab rose or lavender oil on your candle.

Sweet as a blessing from up above
I ask the gods to send me love
A child's hug so warm and pure
Family's love that does endure
Passion's fire, a strong embrace
The love of a friend, true and chaste
I open my heart to the love I need
Love in word and love in deed
I pledge to give love in return
Blooming with the love I earn

Afterward: Be sure to check in with your heart chakra periodically to make sure it is still open and ready for love!

—Deborah Blake

☽ Saturday
4th ♈
☽ enters ♉ 12:05 am
New Moon 3:18 am
Color: Gray

Flidais, an Irish goddess, oversees forests and all wild things

---

22 Sunday
1st ♉
☽ v/c 1:10 pm
Color: Orange

Earth Day; the first Earth Day was in 1970

April

23 Monday
1st ☿
☽ enters ♊ 1:05 pm
Color: Lavender

The Wiccan pentacle is officially added to the
Veterans Administration's list of approved emblems
for memorials, markers, and gravestones, 2007

First National All-Woman Conference on
Women's Spirituality held, Boston, 1976

24 Tuesday
1st ♊
Color: Black

25 Wednesday
1st ♊
☽ v/c 4:31 pm
Color: Topaz

USA Today reports that Patricia Hutchins
is the first military Wiccan granted
religious leave for the sabbats, 1989

26 Thursday
1st ♊
☽ enters ♋ 1:42 am
Color: White

Take care with ladybugs, as killing one can bring bad luck

27 Friday
1st ♋
Color: Purple

Set in Eastern Daylight Time (EDT)

Beltaine

The Feast of Beltaine marks the beginning of the bright half of the year. At this time, the herds and flocks are moved from the village up into the hills and mountains, where they will have fresh grazing all summer long. It was a time to celebrate and to preserve the abundance and fertility of the earth and its creatures.

Huge bonfires were created from nine types of sacred wood, and the animals were run between two fires to protect them. People also passed between the fires—some even jumped over the Beltaine fires—for protection and good fortune. Wildflowers, especially yellow ones, were gathered and brought into the home. Healing plants picked at dawn on Beltaine were believed to have great power.

On Beltaine, light two candles—yellow, white, or green—and place them on two separate tables or altars. Decorate the altars with freshly gathered spring flowers and place a plate of sacred cakes nearby for the gods and goddesses. Circle the tables three times, sunwise, thanking the gods for their blessings and abundance. Then walk between the candles for protection and good fortune to ensure your prayers are received by the Ancient Ones.

—Sharynne MacLeod NicMhacha

28 Saturday

1st ♋
☽ v/c 3:05 am
☽ enters ♌ 12:10 pm
Color: Blue

The earthy, spicy notes of patchouli incense boost sensuality and fertility

☽ Sunday

1st ♌
2nd quarter 5:57 am
Color: Yellow

Birthday of Ed Fitch, Wiccan author

30 Monday

2nd ♌
☽ v/c 10:17 am
⚷ enters ♉ 12:48 pm
☽ enters ♍ 7:02 pm
Color: Gray

Walpurgis Night; traditionally the
German Witches gather on the Blocksberg, a
mountain in northeastern Germany

1 Tuesday

2nd ♍
Color: Black

Beltane/May Day
Order of the Illuminati formed in
Bavaria by Adam Weishaupt, 1776

2 Wednesday

2nd ♍
☽ v/c 6:58 am
☽ enters ♎ 10:04 pm
Color: Yellow

3 Thursday

2nd ♎
Color: Green

Birthday of D. J. Conway, Wiccan author

4 Friday

2nd ♎
☽ v/c 2:02 pm
☽ enters ♏ 10:20 pm
Color: Purple

The *New York Herald Tribune*
carries the story of a woman who
brought her neighbor to court on
a charge of bewitchment, 1895

The Healing Scorpion Moon

The venom of a scorpion can be deadly. Similarly, the stinging sarcasm of Scorpio hits frighteningly close to home. But like the Egyptian goddess Serket (her name means both "She who tightens the throat" and "She who causes the throat to breathe"), what hurts us can also heal us. In fact, scorpion venom has long been deemed an analgesic by the Chinese and is now being studied in Egypt as a painkiller.

On this Scorpio Full Moon, have the courage to move through pain into healing and strength. Take some time for an uninterrupted Scorpion meditation. Think about a painful personal experience. Start small, with a fairly minor hurt, and move up gradually to more difficult situations. Close your eyes and breathe deeply. Imagine walking through a desert with scrub bushes, cacti, and many different sizes of rocks. One small rock draws your attention—you turn it over to find a scorpion that stings you. The sting evokes all the memories and the pain of that experience you called to mind. Allow the pain to pass through you without resistance. How did you survive? What did you learn? How can it make you stronger? Feel resilience and strength fill your being as your healing begins.

—Kristin Madden

☺ Saturday

2nd ♏

Full Moon 11:35 pm

Color: Black

Cinco de Mayo

Flower Moon

Beltane crossquarter day
(Sun reaches 15° Taurus)

---

6 Sunday

3rd ♏

☽ v/c 8:14 am

☽ enters ♐ 9:39 pm

Color: Gold

Long Island Church of Aphrodite
formed by Reverend Gleb Botkin, 1938

May

7 Monday

3rd ♐
Color: White

Carry a dried peach leaf to improve concentration
while studying and to score well on tests

8 Tuesday

3rd ♐
☽ v/c 9:34 pm
☽ enters ♑ 10:00 pm
Color: Gray

9 Wednesday

3rd ♑
☿ enters ♉ 1:14 am
Color: Yellow

Joan of Arc canonized, 1920

First day of the Lemuria, a Roman festival of the dead;
this festival was probably borrowed from the Etruscans
and is one possible ancestor of our modern Halloween

10 Thursday

3rd ♑
☽ v/c 3:11 pm
Color: Turquoise

Census Day (Canada)

11 Friday

3rd ♑
☽ enters ♒ 1:03 am
Color: Rose

Massachusetts Bay Colony Puritans
ban Christmas celebrations
because they are too Pagan, 1659

Set in Eastern Daylight Time (EDT)

Sweet Delight Shake

1 ripe banana, peeled
1 cup frozen strawberries
1 cup milk: soy, almond, or cow's
½ tsp. vanilla extract
1 tsp. ground flax seed
1 T. protein powder (I prefer
   soy protein, but you can also
   use whey powder.)

In a blender, place the banana representing sweet desire, and the strawberries for wild delight. Red and white are the traditional colors of Beltane. Add all other ingredients and blend on high for one minute. Imagine the red and white wrapping around and around like maypole ribbons, weaving sweet desire with wild delight.

Pour into a tall glass, and garnish with a simple slice of banana before serving. This recipe makes two large delight-filled shakes.

Complete with protein, essential fatty acids from the flax seeds, antioxidants and phyto-nutrients, this Sweet Delight Shake will give you the nutritional power to celebrate the awakening of the Earth and the union of God and Goddess, in whatever delicious way you want. Go ahead, create your own "sweet delight."

—Dallas Jennifer Cobb

○ **Saturday**
3rd ≈
4th quarter 5:47 pm
☽ v/c 8:52 pm
Color: Blue

As a totem, otter teaches play and cheerfulness;
it's ideal for people who work with children

---

13 Sunday
4th ≈
☽ enters ♓ 7:42 am
Color: Orange

Mother's Day
Celtic Tree Month of Hawthorn begins

May

14 Monday

4th ♓
Color: Lavender

Widow Robinson of Kidderminster
and her two daughters are arrested for
trying to prevent the return of Charles II
from exile by use of magic, 1660

15 Tuesday

4th ♓
☽ v/c 7:59 am
♀ ℞ 10:33 am
☽ enters ♈ 5:45 pm
Color: Red

16 Wednesday

4th ♈
Color: Brown

*Brides go veiled to protect them
from malicious spirits that look
for happy people to molest*

17 Thursday

4th ♈
✳ enters ♏ 2:15 am
☽ v/c 5:44 pm
Color: Crimson

18 Friday

4th ♈
♀ enters ♈ 12:18 am
☽ enters ♉ 6:03 am
Color: Coral

The color white is associated with the Child God and beginnings

19 Saturday

4th ♉

Color: Black

An eclipse (solar or lunar) is an abrupt,
radical change—the best opportunity to
get out of a rut or break a bad habit

☽ Sunday

4th ♉

☽ v/c 8:35 am

☉ enters ♊ 11:16 am

☽ enters ♊ 7:05 pm

New Moon 7:47 pm

Color: Yellow

Sun enters Gemini

Solar eclipse 7:23 pm, 0° ♊ 21'

Set in Eastern Daylight Time (EDT)

May

21 Monday
1st ♊
Color: Gray

Birthday of Gwydion Pendderwen,
Pagan bard, 1946

22 Tuesday
1st ♊
☽ v/c 6:51 pm
Color: Red

Adoption of the Earth Religion
Anti-Abuse Act, 1988

23 Wednesday
1st ♊
☽ enters ♋ 7:31 am
Color: Brown

Work with tektite for assistance in radical transformation

24 Thursday
1st ♋
☿ enters ♊ 7:12 am
Color: Green

25 Friday
1st ♋
☽ v/c 10:34 am
☽ enters ♌ 6:11 pm
Color: White

Scott Cunningham initiated into the
Traditional Gwyddonic Order of the Wicca, 1981

Set in Eastern Daylight Time (EDT)

Energy & Light

To tap into the energy and light of summer, light a yellow candle and concentrate on the power of the sun above. Do this spell at noon, if possible. If you can be outside, all the better. Stretch your arms upward to take in all that great energy as you say the spell.

The sun is high
The sky is bright
I call on energy and light
To lift my soul
To fill me up
To god and goddess, raise the cup
Summer sunshine
Filled with cheer
Laughter, joy, and friendship near
Dancing, singing
In the sunshine
Energy and light be mine
　　　　　　　　—Deborah Blake

---

26 Saturday
1st ♌
Color: Brown

A moth totem brings subtlety and hidden knowledge, often through dreams

27 Sunday
1st ♌
☽ v/c 7:54 pm
Color: Orange

Shavuot
Birthday of Morning Glory
Zell-Ravenheart, Church of All Worlds
Final confession of witchcraft by
Isobel Gowdie, Scotland, 1662

May/June

○ Monday
1st ♌
☽ enters ♍ 2:06 am
2nd quarter 4:16 pm
Color: Ivory

Memorial Day (observed)

29 Tuesday
2nd ♍
Color: White

Bloodroot strengthens family ties and encourages respect

30 Wednesday
2nd ♍
☽ v/c 1:50 am
☽ enters ♎ 6:46 am
Color: White

Death of Joan of Arc, 1431

31 Thursday
2nd ♎
☽ v/c 9:31 pm
Color: Purple

1 Friday

2nd ♎
☽ enters ♏ 8:31 am
Color: Rose

Witchcraft Act of 1563 takes effect in England

Set in Eastern Daylight Time (EDT)

2 Saturday

2nd ♏
Color: Indigo

Birthday of Alessandro
di Cagliostro, magician, 1743

3 Sunday

2nd ♏
☽ v/c 5:29 am
☽ enters ♐ 8:32 am
Color: Amber

June

☺ Monday

2nd ♐
Full Moon 7:12 am
♆ ℞ 5:03 pm
Color: Lavender

Strong Sun Moon
Lunar eclipse 7:03 am, 14° ♐ 08'

5 Tuesday

3rd ♐
☽ v/c 1:08 am
☽ enters ♑ 8:31 am
Color: Red

For purifying the body and aiding tissue regeneration, use peridot

6 Wednesday

3rd ♑
Color: Topaz

*In Norse cosmology Borghild,
the goddess of the moon and evening
mist, slays the Sun at the end of each day*

7 Thursday

3rd ♑
☿ enters ♋ 7:16 am
☽ v/c 8:38 am
☽ enters ♒ 10:17 am
Color: Green

8 Friday

3rd ♒
Color: White

The horse totem grants safe travel and connection with the land

Set in Eastern Daylight Time (EDT)

The Pathfinding Horse Moon

The horse has symbolized raw power and riches to people across the globe. This noble beast has allowed us to travel at great speeds, giving us greater freedom to explore our world. Horses have carried us to new lands and into remote areas of our own. The horse is also a common journeying guide, including the psychopompic journey, and is often seen as the otherworldly steed of the shaman.

This Full Moon is in Sagittarius, symbolized by the dual nature of the centaur and a good deal of horse energy. A great astrologer once described this apparent conflict within Sagittarius not as a struggle between two natures, but as a choice of directions.

To explore your path and any new directions you might take, you will need a pendulum (a ring on a string will do), and your life-adventure map. Create your map by drawing a large circle on a piece of paper. Divide the circle into a pie graph, with one section representing your current path. Into the other sections, place your potential paths, hopes, and dreams. Take your pendulum and ask what paths are most aligned to financial, academic, spiritual, or emotional success, then let the pendulum help find your direction.

—Kristin Madden

---

9 Saturday

3rd ≈
☽ v/c 2:33 pm
☽ enters ♓ 3:22 pm
Color: Black

Birthday of Grace Cook, medium and
founder of the White Eagle Lodge, 1892

---

10 Sunday

3rd ♓
Color: Amber

Celtic Tree Month of Oak begins
Hanging of Bridget Bishop, first to
die in the Salem Witch trials, 1692

June

◯ Monday

3rd ♓
☽ v/c 6:41 am
4th quarter 6:41 am
♃ enters ♊ 1:22 pm
Color: Ivory

*Magic involving abundance and
opulence is ideal for summer*

12 Tuesday

4th ♓
☽ enters ♈ 12:21 am
♀ ℞ 1:12 am
Color: Red

13 Wednesday

4th ♈
☽ v/c 11:09 pm
Color: White

Birthday of William Butler Yeats, poet and
member of the Golden Dawn, 1865
Birthday of Gerald Gardner, founder
of the Gardnerian tradition, 1884

14 Thursday

4th ♈
☽ enters ♉ 12:22 pm
Color: Turquoise

Flag Day

15 Friday

4th ♉
Color: Purple

Margaret Jones becomes the first person executed as a Witch in
the Massachusetts Bay Colony, 1648; she was a Boston doctor
who was accused of witchcraft after several of her patients died

Sun God Supreme

1 cup flour
1 tsp. baking powder
¼ tsp. baking soda
2 T. of melted butter or oil
1 egg
¾ cup yogurt
Garnish with 3 cups cubed fruit, all colors

Sift dry ingredients together. Then separately whisk wet ingredients together. Combine wet and dry, mixing for no more than 20 strokes, one for each day of June until the solstice. Let mixture sit for 10 minutes while you prepare fruit, set the table, and heat a frying pan lightly coated with oil or butter on medium heat.

Pour batter into sun-shaped disks. Cook until bubbles that have formed in the batter burst and make little dry craters. Flip once and briefly cook the other side. Serve on brightly colored plates surrounded by fruit of all colors, which represents the abundant growth and glory of the Earth Goddess. Drizzle with honey or maple syrup and enjoy.

Pancakes combine the traditional foords of Litha—butter, milk, cakes, and honey—and represent the Sun God at the height of his reign.

—Dallas Jennifer Cobb

---

16 Saturday

4th ♉
☽ v/c 8:09 am
Color: Brown

---

17 Sunday

4th ♉
☽ enters ♊ 1:24 am
Color: Yellow

Father's Day
Birthday of Starhawk, Wiccan author

June

18 Monday
4th ♊
Color: Silver

Church of All Worlds
chartered with the IRS, 1970

Tuesday
4th ♊
☽ v/c 11:02 am
New Moon 11:02 am
☽ enters ♋ 1:34 pm
Color: Maroon

Fir wood grants long, clear vision

20 Wednesday
1st ♋
☉ enters ♋ 7:09 pm
Color: Brown

Sun enters Cancer
Midsummer/Litha/Summer Solstice

21 Thursday
1st ♋
☽ v/c 12:48 pm
☽ enters ♌ 11:47 pm
Color: White

22 Friday
1st ♌
Color: Rose

Final witchcraft law in
England repealed, 1951

Set in Eastern Daylight Time (EDT)

Midsummer

Summer Solstice is a time for joyous celebration, when we revel in the greenness and bounty of the earth. Feasts and dancing often took place at this time, and huge wooden or wickerwork wheels were set alight and rolled down hills to imitate the movement of the Sun. At solstice, we celebrate this expansive time of abundance, power, and possibility.

Solstice bonfires were lit in many areas, and sacred herbs like mugwort and vervain were tossed into the flames. Rings or chaplets of summer flowers were worn on the head and the community came together for festive rituals and revelry. Sacred rituals were held to mark this astronomical and earthly event. In very ancient times, some ceremonies likely took place inside stone circles that were aligned with the solstices and equinoxes.

At the solstice, take some time away from the hustle and bustle of everyday life to revel in the earth's beauty and the glory of the Sun's golden light. Visit a body of water or sacred woods and make some garlands or chaplets of summer flowers—including one of yourself. Give thanks by making a libation of cider or ale for the spirits of the natural world.

—Sharynne MacLeod NicMhacha

23 Saturday
1st ♌
☽ v/c 6:26 pm
♀ enters ♊ 6:52 pm
Color: Gray

24 Sunday
1st ♌
☽ enters ♍ 7:42 am
Color: Orange

Birthday of Janet Farrar, Wiccan author
James I Witchcraft Statute of 1604 is replaced in 1763 with a law against pretending to practice divination and witchcraft; law stands until 1951

June/July

25 Monday
1st ♍
♄ D 4:00 am
☿ enters ♌ 10:24 pm
Color: Gray

A law is introduced in Germany by
Archbishop Siegfried III to encourage
conversion rather than burning of heretics, 1233

○ Tuesday
1st ♍
☽ v/c 6:53 am
☽ enters ♎ 1:15 pm
2nd quarter 11:30 pm
Color: Black

Richard of Gloucester assumes the English throne after
accusing the widowed queen of Edward IV of witchcraft, 1483

27 Wednesday
2nd ♎
♀ D 11:07 am
Color: Yellow

Birthday of Scott Cunningham,
Wiccan author, 1956

28 Thursday
2nd ♎
☽ v/c 4:22 am
☽ enters ♏ 4:32 pm
Color: Crimson

Birthday of Stewart Farrar, Wiccan author

29 Friday
2nd ♏
Color: Coral

Set in Eastern Daylight Time (EDT)

30 Saturday

2nd ♏

☽ v/c 3:46 pm
☽ enters ♐ 6:04 pm
Color: Blue

1 Sunday

2nd ♐
Color: Amber

To discourage an unwanted visitor from
returning, sweep the room they were in
immediately after they leave

July

2 Monday
2nd ♐
☽ v/c 6:21 pm
☽ enters ♑ 6:51 pm
Color: White

*The raven totem conveys alertness,
cunning, and connection to the sky*

☺ Tuesday
2nd ♑
♂ enters ♎ 8:32 am
Full Moon 2:52 pm
Color: Maroon

Blessing Moon
Trial of Joan Prentice, who was accused
of sending an imp in the form of a
ferret to bite children; she allegedly had
two imps named Jack and Jill, 1549

4 Wednesday

3rd ♑
☽ v/c 8:25 am
☽ enters ♒ 8:26 pm
Color: Yellow

Independence Day

5 Thursday

3rd ♒
Color: Turquoise

Conviction of Witches at third of four
famous trials at Chelmsford, England, 1589

6 Friday

3rd ♒
☽ v/c 11:49 am
Color: Coral

Scott Cunningham is initiated into
Ancient Pictish Gaelic Way, 1981

Set in Eastern Daylight Time (EDT)

The Successful Goat Moon

The Capricorn Full Moon is aligned with the mountain goat that, slowly but surely, climbs the highest mountains. Even as youngsters, they are agile on their feet and learn what is needed to thrive in the most challenging environments. They are in tune with the earth and seem to intuitively know the right paths to stay safe and reach their goals.

In keeping with the earthy, practical energy of this Moon, make a list of your top five goals and dreams. Rate them from one (not much) to three (very much) according to how possible you believe it to be and how much time you spend actually working toward it. Those goals with the lowest scores have the least amount of energy going into them. If these are important to you, you need to find ways to create small successes that will build belief and bring them closer to fruition. Consider the time you spend on all of your dreams. Is this time well spent? Are you following the path that leads you up the mountain, or are you simply jumping from rock to rock and getting nowhere? Make a concrete plan to attain your most important goals. Once you have a plan, you must step onto the path and begin to climb.

—Kristin Madden

7 Saturday

3rd ≈
☽ enters ♓ 12:29 am
Color: Gray

8 Sunday

3rd ♓
☽ v/c 7:00 am
Color: Orange

Celtic Tree Month of Holly begins

July

9 Monday

3rd ♓
☽ enters ♈ 8:14 am
⚳ enters ♊ 5:25 pm
Color: Gray

Death of Herman Slater,
proprietor of Magickal Childe
bookstore in New York, 1992
Birthday of Amber K, Wiccan author

☽ Tuesday

3rd ♈
4th quarter 9:48 pm
Color: Red

*Dusk brings the shadows and the night,
ideal for working with hidden things and intuition*

11 Wednesday

4th ♈
☽ v/c 5:23 am
☽ enters ♉ 7:30 pm
Color: Topaz

12 Thursday

4th ♉
Color: Green

Cleansing with eucalyptus removes evil energy after contact

13 Friday

4th ♉
♅ ℞ 5:49 am
☽ v/c 3:46 pm
Color: Pink

Birthday of Dr. John Dee, magician, 1527

Set in Eastern Daylight Time (EDT)

Abundance & Prosperity

To tap into the growth and energy of summer and bring abundance and prosperity into your life, light a green candle. Use mint oil on the candle or chew a sprig of the herb to give the spell a boost. Visualize yourself getting all the things you need and want (within reason).

The earth bursts forth with
    abundance
      As above, so below
The sky overflows with light
      As above, so below
Increase and bounty are all around me
      As above, so below
Everything is green and growing
      As above, so below
Abundance and prosperity are mine
In the best possible ways
      As above, so below
And so it is

        —Deborah Blake

---

14 Saturday

4th ♉
☽ enters ♊ 8:26 am
☿ ℞ 10:16 pm
Color: Indigo

First crop circles recorded
on Silbury Hill, 1988

---

15 Sunday

4th ♊
Color: Gold

July

16 Monday

4th ♊
☽ v/c 6:56 am
☿ D 6:57 am
☽ enters ♋ 8:31 pm
Color: Ivory

*A crescent can represent either youth
(waxing moon) or age (waning moon)*

---

17 Tuesday

4th ♋
Color: Red

First airing of *The Witching Hour*, a
Pagan radio show hosted by Winter
Wren and Don Lewis, on station
WONX in Evanston, Illinois, 1992

---

18 Wednesday

4th ♋
Color: Brown

☽ Thursday

4th ♋
☽ v/c 12:24 am
New Moon 12:24 am
☽ enters ♌ 6:13 am
Color: Crimson

Rebecca Nurse hanged in
Salem, Massachusetts, 1692

---

20 Friday

1st ♌
Color: Coral

Ramadan begins

Pope Adrian VI issues a papal bull to the
Inquisition to re-emphasize the 1503
bull of Julius II calling for the purging
of "sorcerers by fire and sword," 1523

Set in Eastern Daylight Time (EDT)

21 Saturday
1st ♌
☽ v/c 1:17 am
☽ enters ♍ 1:24 pm
Color: Blue

22 Sunday
1st ♍
☉ enters ♌ 6:01 am
☽ v/c 8:44 pm
Color: Yellow

Sun enters Leo
Northamptonshire Witches
condemned, 1612
First modern recorded sighting
of the Loch Ness monster, 1930

July

23 Monday
1st ♍
☽ enters ♎ 6:38 pm
Color: White

Use holly wood in spells relating to sleep or rest

24 Tuesday
1st ♎
Color: Black

25 Wednesday
1st ♎
☽ v/c 11:22 am
☽ enters ♏ 10:29 pm
Color: Yellow

Death of Pope Innocent VIII, who issued bull
Summis Desiderantes Affectibus, 1492

○ Thursday
1st ♏
2nd quarter 4:56 am
☽ v/c 11:38 am
Color: Purple

Confession of Chelmsford Witches at first of
four famous trials at Chelmsford, 1566; the
others were held in 1579, 1589, and 1645;
"Witch Finder General" Matthew Hopkins
presided at the 1645 trials

27 Friday
2nd ♏
Color: Purple

Jennet Preston becomes the first of the
"Malkin Tower" Witches to be hanged, 1612;
she was convicted of hiring Witches
to help her murder Thomas Lister

Set in Eastern Daylight Time (EDT)

Lughnasadh

Lughnasadh was celebrated by the pagan Celts and was the time of a sacred harvest festival. The name of the holiday means the "Feast of the God Lugh," who instituted the holiday to commemorate his foster mother Tailtiu. Legends tell how she died from the exertion of clearing many plains to prepare the ground for crops and grain.

All over Europe, people celebrated the beginning of the sacred harvest. If the grain was not yet ripe, a sheaf was symbolically cut at this sacred time to ensure that the entire harvest would go well. Harvest feasts were prepared, and corn dollies were created. Sacred cakes were made as offerings to the gods. It was a time of festivity and thanksgiving.

At Lughnasadh, take some time to think about all the blessings you have been given, as well as those blessings you hope to reap in the seasons to come. Create sacred cakes from grains that your ancestors ate—spelt, oats, and barley are traditional—and place these on an altar decorated with grain or corn, and red and yellow summer flowers. Lugh was a god of wisdom and skill, and can be invoked at this time to bring your dreams into fruition.

—Sharynne MacLeod NicMhacha

---

28 Saturday
2nd ♏
☽ enters ♐ 1:18 am
Color: Black

---

29 Sunday
2nd ♐
☽ v/c 5:01 pm
Color: Orange

Agnes Waterhouse, one of the Chelmsford Witches, is hanged under the new witchcraft statute of Elizabeth I, 1566; she was accused of having a spotted cat familiar named Sathan

---

July/August

30 Monday
2nd ♐
☽ enters ♑ 3:29 am
♀ ℞ 6:30 pm
Color: Silver

Conrad of Marburg is murdered on the open
road, presumably because he had shifted from
persecuting poor heretics to nobles, 1233

31 Tuesday
2nd ♑
☽ v/c 7:30 pm
Color: Gray

Birthday of H. P. Blavatsky, founder
of the Theosophical Society, 1831

Date of fabled meeting of British
Witches to raise cone of power to stop
Hitler's invasion of England, 1940

☻ Wednesday
2nd ♑
☽ enters ♒ 5:56 am
Full Moon 11:27 pm
Color: White

Corn Moon
Lammas/Lughnasadh
Birthday of Edward Kelley,
medium of Dr. John Dee, 1555
AURORA Network UK founded, 2000

2 Thursday
3rd ♒
Color: Green

Birthday of Henry Steel Olcott,
who cofounded the Theosophical
Society with H. P. Blavatsky, 1832

3 Friday
3rd ♒
☽ v/c 3:24 am
☽ enters ♓ 9:58 am
Color: White

The Dreaming Heron Moon

Like the heron, this Aquarius Full Moon brings the energies of both air and water. Birds of the betwixt and between, most herons hunt at dusk and dawn, along the edge of water and land. In parts of Africa, the heron was believed to communicate with the gods. The Greek goddess Athena used a heron as a divine messenger. This bird can lead us through the veil between worlds and allow us to commune with the Divine.

Before you go to bed, pour yourself a small glass of water. Consider a situation you need to resolve or a question you want answered. Clarify the question or situation as much as possible, then take up the glass of water between both hands. Hold it up to your third eye and send the question or request for resolution into the water. Ask for insight and clarity during dreaming and tell yourself that you will remember any relevant dreams. See and feel this energy permeate the water. Then drink it all. Immediately lie down, relax your body and mind, and go to sleep. Keep a pen and paper beside your bed and with you throughout the next day. Repeat the process if you need practice working with dreaming or need additional insight.

—Kristin Madden

4 Saturday

3rd ♓
Color: Blue

Smoky quartz connects the metaphysical and
physical realms; use it to manifest dreams and ideals

5 Sunday

3rd ♓
☽ v/c 1:56 pm
☽ enters ♈ 4:59 pm
Color: Gold

Celtic Tree Month of Hazel begins

August

6 Monday

3rd ♈
Color: Ivory

A meteor shower brings unexpected opportunities;
don't miss yours—quick, make a wish!

7 Tuesday

3rd ♈
♀ enters ♋ 9:43 am
☽ v/c 4:04 pm
Color: Red

Lammas crossquarter day
(Sun reaches 15° Leo)

8 Wednesday

3rd ♈
☿ D 1:40 am
☽ enters ♉ 3:28 am
Color: Brown

◯ Thursday

3rd ♉
☽ v/c 2:55 pm
4th quarter 2:55 pm
Color: White

For loyalty and good health, work with the hound totem

10 Friday

4th ♉
☽ enters ♊ 4:11 pm
Color: Rose

Set in Eastern Daylight Time (EDT)

Presto Pesto Pasta

3 cups fresh basil
1½ cups chopped walnuts
4 cloves garlic, minced
¼ cup grated goat or sheep
    Romano cheese
½ cup olive oil
Salt and pepper to taste
16–24 ounces pasta (4 servings)
4 cups chopped vegetables

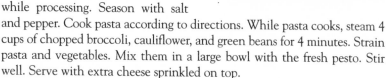

In a food processor, blend basil, nuts, garlic, and cheese. Add oil slowly while processing. Season with salt and pepper. Cook pasta according to directions. While pasta cooks, steam 4 cups of chopped broccoli, cauliflower, and green beans for 4 minutes. Strain pasta and vegetables. Mix them in a large bowl with the fresh pesto. Stir well. Serve with extra cheese sprinkled on top.

Pesto-based dishes befit Lammas because basil has the spiritual qualities of protection and love—excellent energies to fill ourselves with as we turn slowly and quietly toward the coming darkness. For added protein, steam 2 cups of frozen shrimp for 4 minutes and serve on top, or mixed in. The shrimp represent the Sun God's drooping strength.

—Dallas Jennifer Cobb

11 Saturday

4th ♊
Color: Blue

Laurie Cabot withdraws from Salem,
Massachusetts, mayoral race, 1987
Birthday of Edain McCoy, Wiccan author

12 Sunday

4th ♊
☽ v/c 5:49 pm
Color: Orange

August

13 Monday
4th ♊
☽ enters ♋ 4:27 am
Color: Lavender

Aradia de Toscano allegedly
born in Volterra, Italy, 1313
Church of Wicca founded in Australia
by Lady Tamara Von Forslun, 1989

14 Tuesday
4th ♋
Color: Scarlet

*Look to the wasp totem for a model of order
and productivity, backed by fierce defenses*

15 Wednesday
4th ♋
☽ v/c 4:21 am
☽ enters ♌ 2:05 pm
Color: Topaz

Birthday of Charles Godfrey Leland,
author of *Aradia, Gospel of Witches*, 1824

16 Thursday
4th ♌
Color: Green

☽ Friday
4th ♌
New Moon 11:54 am
☽ v/c 1:55 pm
☽ enters ♍ 8:33 pm
Color: Pink

Scott Cunningham's first
initiation into Wicca, 1973

Set in Eastern Daylight Time (EDT)

Reaping the Harvest

To start reaping those things that you planted the seeds for earlier in the year, light a green or brown candle—if possible, under the Full Moon. Place some flowers or fruit on the altar along with your list of "seeds" from March, if you still have it.

Seeds were planted
Watered, tended
Soil was turned
And fences mended
Long I've worked
For harvest's treasure
And I'll reap it
Now with pleasure
As the season's wheel does turn
I shall reap all that I earn

Afterward: Start taking concrete steps toward completing goals you started earlier in the year. Now is the time to finish what you started, if you can.

—Deborah Blake

18 Saturday
1st ♍
☽ v/c 7:26 pm
Color: Black

Father Urbain Grandier found guilty of bewitching nuns at a convent in Loudoun, France, 1634

19 Sunday
1st ♍
Color: Yellow

Ramadan ends
John Willard and Reverend George Burroughs put to death in the Salem Witch trials, 1692

August

20 Monday
1st ♍
☽ enters ♎ 12:45 am
Color: Silver

Execution of Lancashire Witches, 1612

Birthday of H. P. Lovecraft, horror
writer and alleged magician, 1890

Birthday of Ann Moura, author and Witch

21 Tuesday
1st ♎
Color: Gray

22 Wednesday

1st ♎
☽ v/c 3:13 am
☽ enters ♏ 3:54 am
☉ enters ♍ 1:07 pm
Color: Brown

Sun enters Virgo

Pope John XXII orders the Inquisition at
Carcassonne to seize the property of Witches,
sorcerers, and those who make wax images, 1320

23 Thursday

1st ♏
☽ v/c 5:34 am
♂ enters ♏ 11:24 am
Color: Turquoise

◑ Friday
1st ♏
☽ enters ♐ 6:50 am
2nd quarter 9:54 am
Color: Coral

Burn larch wood to repel evil spirits with its protective smoke

Set in Eastern Daylight Time (EDT)

25 Saturday

2nd ♐
Color: Brown

If a ceremonial candle blows out (and there is not a noticeable wind) it indicates malicious spirits nearby

26 Sunday

2nd ♐
☽ v/c 2:39 am
☽ enters ♑ 9:58 am
Color: Gold

August/September

27 Monday

2nd ♑
Color: Ivory

The color gold corresponds to revelations and intelligence

28 Tuesday

2nd ♑
☽ v/c 6:33 am
☽ enters ♒ 1:38 pm
Color: Red

The Aztec moon god is Tecciztecatl, whose name means
He from the Innermost Twist of the Conch Shell

29 Wednesday

2nd ♒
Color: Topaz

Election of Pope Innocent VIII, who issued the
papal bull Summis Desiderantes Affectibus, 1484

30 Thursday

2nd ♒
☽ v/c 1:48 pm
☽ enters ♓ 6:31 pm
Color: Purple

☺ Friday

2nd ♓
Full Moon 9:58 am
☿ enters ♍ 10:32 pm
Color: Purple

Blue Moon
Birthday of Raymond Buckland,
who, along with his first wife, Rosemary,
is generally credited with bringing
Gardnerian Wicca to the United States

Set in Eastern Daylight Time (EDT)

The Wise Blue Salmon Moon

In the Celtic tradition, Bradan, the salmon, is the oldest of all animals. Bradan feasted on the nuts of nine hazel trees growing around the well of wisdom, the Well of Segais. The tale of Fionn mac Cumhaill tells of a young boy given the task of watching over the cooking of the Salmon of Wisdom. A splash of hot juice from the pot caused the boy to stick his burning finger in his mouth, imparting all the knowledge and wisdom to the boy, who was renamed Fionn.

Seek wisdom and oneness on this Pisces Blue Moon. Fill a shallow bowl, with no inside markings, with pure water. Sprinkle a touch of ground hazelnut, hazelnut liquor, or hazelnut flavoring on top. Pass your left hand, then your right hand over the water, attuning yourself to its energy. Still your mind and allow your experience of Self to expand to include everything in every reality. Continue to expand your awareness until your current identity is just one small part of who you are. Tell yourself that you encompass all things and that you will retain some of this wisdom when you return to your body. When you are ready, gradually return to normal awareness.

—Kristin Madden

---

1 Saturday
3rd ♓
☽ v/c 4:02 pm
Color: Gray

---

2 Sunday
3rd ♓
☽ enters ♈ 1:37 am
Color: Orange

Celtic Tree Month of Vine begins
Birthday of Reverend Paul
Beyerl, Wiccan author

September

3 Monday
3rd ♈
Color: Lavender

Labor Day

4 Tuesday
3rd ♈
☽ v/c 7:06 am
☽ enters ♉ 11:41 am
Color: Black

Reap what you have sown with
success and wealth spells in autumn

5 Wednesday
3rd ♉
☽ v/c 2:54 pm
Color: Yellow

The hexagram stands for unity, divinity, and balance

6 Thursday
3rd ♉
♀ enters ♌ 10:48 am
Color: Green

7 Friday
3rd ♉
☽ enters ♊ 12:10 am
Color: Pink

Founding of the Theosophical
Society by H. P. Blavatsky, Henry
Steel Olcott, and others, 1875

Set in Eastern Daylight Time (EDT)

Balance

To bring more balance into your life, burn a black candle and a white candle. If you want, place a tarot card on your altar that symbolizes balance to you (I like to use the Wheel of Fortune, Justice, Temperance, or my favorite, the Star).

God and goddess
Send me the gift of balance
Help me to make good choices
And to see clearly
As I balance work and play
Home, health, love, and family
Keep me focused and firm
As I walk the difficult path
That is the well-lived life
And lend me your strength and wisdom
So I might have balance
In all these things
So mote it be

—Deborah Blake

◐ Saturday

3rd ♊
4th quarter 9:15 am
Color: Blue

---

9 Sunday

4th ♊
☽ v/c 6:59 am
☽ enters ♋ 12:49 pm
Color: Yellow

September

10 Monday

4th ♋
Color: Silver

Birthday of Carl Llewellyn
Weschcke, owner and president
of Llewellyn Worldwide

11 Tuesday

4th ♋
☽ v/c 5:58 pm
☽ enters ♌ 11:00 pm
Color: Maroon

Birthday of Silver RavenWolf,
Wiccan author

12 Wednesday

4th ♌
Color: Yellow

Amber incense balances emotions and aids meditation

13 Thursday

4th ♌
Color: Crimson

14 Friday

4th ♌
☽ v/c 1:14 am
☽ enters ♍ 5:30 am
Color: Purple

Birthday of Ellen Dugan, Wiccan author
Birthday of Henry Cornelius Agrippa,
scholar and magician, 1486

Set in Eastern Daylight Time (EDT)

Brilliant, Balanced Roasted Vegetables

3 cups potatoes, cubed
1 cup sweet potatoes, cubed
1 cup carrots, cubed
1 green pepper, chopped
1 yellow pepper, chopped
8 cloves garlic, peeled
1 large onion, peeled and chopped
3 tablespoons olive oil
1 tsp. fresh rosemary
1 tsp. fresh sage
1 tsp. sea salt

Combine all vegetables in a large bowl. Pour in oil and mix well. Add herbs and salt, and mix again. Spread on a lightly oiled cookie sheet and bake at 400 degrees F for 20 minutes. Remove and stir vegetables around, then bake for another 20 minutes until crispy and brown.

This dish of brilliant, balanced roasted vegetables honors the waning Sun God and the aging Goddess moving from mother to crone. The traditional colors of brown, orange, yellow, and green in this recipe represent the balance between night and day, and the abundant harvest. A combination of savory and sweet, this recipe brings the best of the season together in one warm dish.

—Dallas Jennifer Cobb

☽ Saturday
4th ♍
New Moon 10:11 pm
Color: Brown

*Salmon is the totem of wisdom
and transformation; it grants
the connection to the sea*

16 Sunday
1st ♍
☽ v/c 7:26 am
☽ enters ♎ 8:55 am
⚴ enters ♐ 1:50 pm
☿ enters ♎ 7:22 pm
Color: Gold

17 Monday
1st ♎
Color: White

Rosh Hashanah
Bewitched debuts on ABC-TV, 1964

18 Tuesday

1st ♎
♇ D 1:07 am
☽ v/c 7:30 am
☽ enters ♏ 10:46 am
Color: Red

19 Wednesday

1st ♏
Color: White

*Use the same pencil or pen while studying and on
the test so it can help you remember the answers*

20 Thursday
1st ♏
☽ v/c 9:11 am
☽ enters ♐ 12:34 pm
Color: Purple

21 Friday
1st ♐
Color: Pink

UN International Day of Peace

Mabon

The season of autumn is in full swing, and the crisp air at nighttime encourages us to savor every moment. Plants of all kinds are ripening—grain, vegetables, fruits—and remind us of the magical bounty of the earth which is all around us.

In some branches of modern earth religion, Autumn Equinox is known as the "Witches' Thanksgiving," and feasts are held to show gratitude and celebrate abundance. This is a good time to share your abundance. Donate some time or goods at a food pantry or soup kitchen, or make a meal for an acquaintance who is going through hard times. They may also appreciate gifts of clothing, books, and ritual items—all forms of recyling which help the Earth maintain balance!

The Autumn Equinox altar is especially rich and poignant, covered with orange, red, and yellow fall leaves; small bundles or sheaves of magical herbs and plants; and apples, gourds, or pumpkins. Red and yellow candles may be lit to deepen ourselves into a place of humility and gratitude, and mulled cider placed in goblets or cauldrons to honor the gods and spirits of the land.

—Sharynne MacLeod NicMhacha

◯ Saturday

1st ♐
☉ enters ♎ 10:49 am
☽ v/c 12:45 pm
☽ enters ♑ 3:20 pm
2nd quarter 3:41 pm
Color: Indigo

Mabon/Fall Equinox
Sun enters Libra

---

23 Sunday

2nd ♑
Color: Amber

Skunk is an ideal totem for pacifists: it teaches awareness, prudence, and effective action

September

24 Monday

2nd ♑
☽ v/c 5:19 pm
☽ enters ♒ 7:32 pm
Color: Gray

As a totem, squirrel is balanced
between above and below, work and play

25 Tuesday

2nd ♒
Color: White

U.S. Senate passes an amendment (705)
attached by Senator Jesse Helms to House
Resolution 3036 (1986 budget bill),
denying tax-exempt status to any organization
that espouses satanism or witchcraft, 1985

26 Wednesday

2nd ♒
♀ enters ♋ 3:00 am
☽ v/c 11:33 pm
Color: Brown

Joan Wiliford hanged at Faversham,
England, 1645; she testified that
the Devil came to her in the form of a black
dog that she called "Bunnie"

27 Thursday

2nd ♒
☽ enters ♓ 1:23 am
Color: White

28 Friday

2nd ♓
☽ v/c 10:35 pm
Color: Coral

Yom Kippur

Set in Eastern Daylight Time (EDT)

The Assertive Ram Moon

We have all seen images of rams butting heads and fighting for their place in the herd. The mating rituals of male sheep can be aggressive, even violent, as rams fight during the rut to determine who gets to mate with the ewes. Rams have also been known to be aggressive outside the breeding season, often to assert dominance.

On this Aries Full Moon, go on a journey to explore your own aggression and assertiveness. Imagine walking toward a meadow. As you enter the meadow, you find yourself surrounded by a large herd of sheep. Suddenly, a ram approaches and challenges you to look him in the eye and hold your ground, if you dare. Take a deep breath and look directly at him. Feel your energy merge with the ram's. You feel his heart pumping in your chest. You feel the horns on your head, and the strong energy that is his. Other animals begin to attract your attention and you charge over to them to explore how you tend to react and the consequences of that response. Once you have explored these experiences, feel yourself separate from the ram. What messages does he impart? Be sure to thank him for sharing himself and teaching you through this experience.

—Kristin Madden

☺ **Saturday**

2nd ♓
☽ enters ♈ 9:14 am
Full Moon 11:19 pm
Color: Black

Harvest Moon

---

30 Sunday

3rd ♈
Color: Yellow

Celtic Tree Month of Ivy begins

October

1 Monday

3rd ♈
☽ v/c 6:32 pm
☽ enters ♉ 7:26 pm
Color: White

Sukkot begins
Birthday of Isaac Bonewits,
Druid, magician, and Witch
Birthday of Annie Besant,
Theosophical Society president, 1847

2 Tuesday

3rd ♉
Color: Scarlet

Birthday of Timothy Roderick,
Wiccan author

3 Wednesday

3rd ♉
♀ enters ♍ 2:59 am
☿ enters ♓ 6:17 pm
Color: White

4 Thursday

3rd ♉
☽ v/c 3:44 am
☽ enters ♊ 7:47 am
♃ ℞ 9:18 am
Color: Purple

President Ronald Reagan signs JR 165, making 1983
"The Year of the Bible" (public law #9728Q); the law
states that the Bible is the word of God and urges a
return to "traditional" Christian values, 1982

5 Friday

3rd ♊
☿ enters ♏ 6:35 am
♄ enters ♏ 4:34 pm
☽ v/c 5:08 pm
Color: Pink

Set in Eastern Daylight Time (EDT)

Banishing Ghosts

To banish the ghosts of all those things that no longer work for you, as we move into the darker season, burn a black candle and smudge yourself with sage. Then visualize your ghosts, (anything or anyone you need to let go of) disappearing into a doorway filled with bright, positive light.

I let go of my ghosts
The things which haunt me
With memories old
The voices that taunt me
I let go of the past
That which makes me weak
And saps my will
Or makes my heart bleak
I banish the dark
Into the long night
I let go of my ghosts
And embrace a new light
So mote it be
—Deborah Blake

---

6 Saturday

3rd ♊
☽ enters ♋ 8:45 pm
♂ enters ♐ 11:21 pm
Color: Black

To explore lives in other times and worlds, use meteorite

---

7 Sunday

3rd ♋
Color: Orange

Birthday of Arnold Crowther, stage magician and Gardnerian Witch, 1909

October

○ Monday

3rd ♋
☽ v/c 3:33 am
4th quarter 3:33 am
Color: Ivory

Sukkot ends
Columbus Day (observed)

9 Tuesday

4th ♋
☽ enters ♌ 7:55 am
Color: Red

*In the forest, the deer totem is a capable guide
on trails and knows the best forage or herbs*

10 Wednesday

4th ♌
☽ v/c 5:40 pm
Color: Topaz

11 Thursday

4th ♌
☽ enters ♍ 3:23 pm
Color: Green

*For grounding or determination
in the face of hard work, wear brown*

12 Friday

4th ♍
☽ v/c 7:48 pm
Color: Rose

Birthday of Aleister Crowley, 1875

13 Saturday
4th ♍
☽ enters ♎ 7:02 pm
Color: Gray

Jacques de Molay and other
French Templars arrested by
order of King Phillip IV, 1306

14 Sunday
4th ♎
Color: Orange

October

☽ Monday
4th ♎
☽ v/c 8:02 am
New Moon 8:02 am
☽ enters ♏ 8:06 pm
Color: White

*Catch a falling leaf before it touches
the ground and you can make a wish*

16 Tuesday
1st ♏
☽ v/c 10:23 pm
Color: Maroon

17 Wednesday
1st ♏
☽ enters ♐ 8:26 pm
Color: Topaz

*Midnight is the peak of lunar magic each night;
use this time for mystical ceremonies or scrying*

18 Thursday
1st ♐
Color: Turquoise

*Birthday of Nicholas Culpeper,
astrologer and herbalist, 1616*

19 Friday
1st ♐
☽ v/c 4:27 pm
☽ enters ♑ 9:41 pm
Color: White

Set in Eastern Daylight Time (EDT)

Gratitude

To say thank you for all the blessings of the past year, light a white candle and make an offering on your altar. (Flowers, food, or drink all work.) Spend a moment thinking about all the things you are grateful for; you can even make a list if you want to remind yourself later of all you have.

Lord and Lady of the light
I give thanks for the blessings
Of the past year
And all that which you have sent me
I am filled with gratitude and appreciation
For the gifts of life and love
Learning and wisdom
Abundance and health
Even when I did not have all I wanted
I had all I needed
And for this I am grateful
And I give thanks for the blessings
And for your light

—Deborah Blake

---

20 Saturday

1st ♑
Color: Indigo

Birthday of Selena Fox, Circle Sanctuary

○ Sunday

1st ♑
♇ ℞ 2:34 am
☽ v/c 11:32 pm
2nd quarter 11:32 pm
Color: Yellow

October

22 Monday

2nd ♑
☽ enters ♒ 1:02 am
☉ enters ♏ 8:14 pm
Color: Lavender

Sun enters Scorpio

23 Tuesday

2nd ♒
☽ v/c 9:27 pm
Color: Black

*The swan totem represents the soul and
guides spirits from one life to the next*

24 Wednesday

2nd ♒
☽ enters ♓ 7:00 am
Color: Yellow

25 Thursday

2nd ♓
Color: White

Jacques de Molay first interrogated
after Templar arrest, 1306

26 Friday

2nd ♓
☽ v/c 11:04 am
☽ enters ♈ 3:31 pm
Color: Pink

De Molay and thirty-one other Templars
confess to heresy in front of an assembly of clergy;
all later recant their confessions, 1306
Sybil Leek, Wiccan author, dies of cancer, 1982

Set in Eastern Daylight Time (EDT)

Samhain

Samhain is an ancient Celtic festival that marked the end of one year and the start of the next. The name means "summer's end" and marks the start of the dark half of the year. The herds now returned to the village, and all plants had to be gathered. All necessary herbs, fruit, nuts, and berries were collected for winter stores.

With the veil between the worlds at its thinnest, interactions between humans and the sacred otherworld often occurred on Samhain. As a New Year's festival, many special ceremonies took place and offerings were made to the gods. Purification rites helped prepare for the year to come. Sacred myths were recited—what had been in the past was being re-created once more. And finally, divination took place to see what was to come.

At Samhain, prepare yourself for the next sacred cycle. Make an oath to the gods to give up or do something special, as an offering. Speak your oath aloud three times in the presence of a sacred flame. Then take a purifying bath and put on your finest garb. Stand before the Old Gods with respect and humility, and ask them to give you a vision to guide you on your path.

—Sharynne MacLeod NicMhacha

---

27 Saturday

2nd ♈
☽ v/c 9:32 pm
Color: Blue

Circle Sanctuary founded, 1974

---

28 Sunday

2nd ♈
♀ enters ♎ 9:04 am
Color: Gold

Celtic Tree Month of Reed begins

October/November

☺ Monday

2nd ♈

☽ enters ♉ 2:15 am
☿ enters ♐ 2:18 am
Full Moon 3:49 pm
☽ v/c 5:01 pm
Color: Gray

Blood Moon
Birthday of Frater Zarathustra,
who founded the Temple of Truth in 1972

30 Tuesday

3rd ♉
Color: Red

PACT (Pagan Awareness Coalition for Teens)
established in Omaha, Nebraska, 2001

31 Wednesday

3rd ♉
♃ ℞ 11:46 am
☽ enters ♊ 2:40 pm
Color: White

Samhain/Halloween
Martin Luther nails his ninety-five theses to
the door of Wittenburg Castle Church,
igniting the Protestant revolution, 1517
Covenant of the Goddess founded, 1975

1 Thursday

3rd ♊
Color: White

All Saints' Day
Aquarian Tabernacle Church established
in the United States, 1979

2 Friday

3rd ♊
☽ v/c 5:21 am
Color: Rose

Circle Sanctuary purchases land
for nature preserve, 1983

The Storytelling Spider Moon

Spider is the weaver, the link to past and future, and the keeper of language and creativity. She bestows her gifts upon writers and poets. Among some cultures, it was she who wove the "primordial alphabet" so that we humans might possess a written language. To some African peoples, Spider is Anansi, the storyteller. He is the Keeper of history and knowledge.

Storytelling can strengthen bonds among family and friends. It can heal and transform individuals. It can also be a fun Halloween game. On this Full Moon, tell your story as a solitary or as a group. Speak it in the third person and make it dramatic, as if you were telling an epic tale of challenge, heroism and love. As a group, pick someone at random to begin. Then go around the circle, with each person adding a sentence or two as you build the story of your community together. Alternatively, make 10 to 20 cards with various words on them. These can be silly words for a fun game or words to evoke insight for a healing story. Sit in a circle and have each person take the same number of cards without looking at them. Go around the circle with each person using one word in a sentence at a time to create humor or healing.

—Kristin Madden

---

3 Saturday

3rd ♊
☽ enters ♋ 3:43 am
Color: Brown

Petronella de Meath, servant of Lady Alice Kyteler,
is executed in the first recorded Witch burning in Ireland, 1324

---

4 Sunday

3rd ♋
☽ v/c 3:37 am
Color: Amber

Daylight Saving Time ends at 2 am

November

5 Monday

3rd ♋
☽ enters ♌ 2:39 pm
Color: Ivory

Traditionally, the cat totem guards the passage to the Otherworld

☽ Tuesday

3rd ♌
☿ ℞ 6:04 pm
4th quarter 7:36 pm
Color: Black

Election Day (general)

7 Wednesday

4th ♌
☽ v/c 10:27 am
☽ enters ♍ 11:35 pm
Color: Topaz

Samhain crossquarter day
(Sun reaches 15° Scorpio)

8 Thursday

4th ♍
Color: Purple

Sentencing of Witches in
Basque Zugarramurdi trial, 1610
Marriage of Patricia and Arnold Crowther,
officiated by Gerald Gardner, 1960

9 Friday

4th ♍
☽ v/c 7:27 pm
Color: Coral

Patricia and Arnold Crowther
married in civil ceremony, 1960

Between-the-Worlds Crumble

Filling
6 apples, cubed
1 cup blackberries
2 T. demerara sugar
½ lemon, juiced

Bottom and Topping
2 cups rolled oats
1 cup whole-wheat flour
1 cup demerara sugar
1 cup butter, melted

Honor life and death with this sweet and sour "candy" recipe that will take you between the worlds. Preheat oven to 350 degrees F. In a medium bowl, mix apples (the God), blackberries that represent the darkness, sugar, and lemon juice. As you stir, watch the darkness of the blackberries color the apples, and say goodbye to the God, who returns to the underworld.

In a large bowl, mix the bottom and topping ingredients. Spread about one-third of this mix across the bottom of a lightly oiled baking dish, and press down with your fingertips to make a dense bottom.

Layer the fruit mixture evenly across. Sprinkle remaining mix on top, covering all of the fruit. Bake for 40 to 45 minutes at 350 degrees F.

—Dallas Jennifer Cobb

10 Saturday
4th ♍
☽ enters ♎ 4:35 am
Color: Blue

11 Sunday
4th ♎
♆ D 2:52 am
Color: Gold

Veterans Day

November

12 Monday

4th ♎
☽ v/c 12:13 am
☽ enters ♏ 6:10 am
Color: Lavender

Libintina is the Roman goddess of funerals

☽ Tuesday

4th ♏
New Moon 5:08 pm
Color: Red

Solar eclipse 5:17 pm, 21° ♏ 57'

14 Wednesday

1st ♏
☿ enters ♏ 2:42 am
☽ v/c 5:39 am
☽ enters ♐ 5:52 am
⚷ D 3:37 pm
Color: Brown

15 Thursday

1st ♐
Color: Turquoise

Islamic New Year
Aquarian Tabernacle Church
established in Canada, 1993

16 Friday

1st ♐
☽ v/c 4:44 am
☽ enters ♑ 5:35 am
♂ enters ♑ 9:36 pm
Color: Pink

Night of Hecate

Set in Eastern Standard Time (EST)

17 Saturday

1st ♑
Color: Black

Birthday of Israel Regardie, occultist
and member of the OTO, 1907

18 Sunday

1st ♑
☽ v/c 12:54 am
☽ enters ♒ 7:10 am
Color: Orange

Aleister Crowley initiated into the
Golden Dawn as Frater Perdurabo, 1898

November

19 Monday
1st ≈
Color: Gray

Birthday of Theodore
Parker Mills, Wiccan elder, 1924

○ Tuesday

1st ≈
☽ v/c 9:31 am
2nd quarter 9:31 am
☽ enters ♓ 11:55 am
☿ D 8:24 pm
Color: Scarlet

Church of All Worlds
incorporates in Australia, 1992

21 Wednesday

2nd ♓
☉ enters ♐ 4:50 pm
♀ enters ♏ 8:20 pm
Color: White

Sun enters Sagittarius

22 Thursday

2nd ♓
☽ v/c 1:32 am
☽ enters ♈ 8:12 pm
Color: Green

Thanksgiving Day
The first pentacle in a VA cemetery is granted
to Patrick Stewart in Nevada; the governor
approved the plaque in the state cemetery
prior to nationwide approval, 2006

23 Friday
2nd ♈
☽ v/c 8:34 pm
Color: Purple

Birthday of Lady Tamara Von Forslun,
founder of the Church of Wicca and the
Aquarian Tabernacle Church in Australia

Set in Eastern Standard Time (EST)

Gifts

To ask for the gifts you would like to receive and start setting the tone for the next year, light a red candle. Feel free to change the words to better suit your own needs. If you want, you can put pictures or symbols on your altar to stand for the gifts you ask for.

As I slip into the silence of winter
I ask for these gifts for the
        year ahead
Prosperity and abundance
For me and my community
Health and well-being
For me and for the land
Balance and productivity
For body and spirit
Love given willingly
And peace most blessed
For me and all the world
In perfect love and perfect trust
                —Deborah Blake

---

24 Saturday
2nd ♈
Color: Brown

---

25 Sunday
2nd ♈
☽ enters ♉ 7:18 am
Color: Yellow

Celtic Tree Month of Elder begins
Dr. John Dee notes Edward
Kelley's death in his diary, 1595

---

26 Monday

2nd ♉
☿ D 5:48 pm
☽ v/c 7:57 pm
Color: Lavender

27 Tuesday

2nd ♉
☽ enters ♊ 7:58 pm
Color: Gray

*The bull stands for strength, endurance, and
stubbornness; a good totem for farmers*

☺ Wednesday

2nd ♊
Full Moon 9:46 am
☽ v/c 8:04 pm
Color: Yellow

Mourning Moon
Lunar eclipse 9:33 am, 6° ♊ 40'

29 Thursday

3rd ♊
Color: White

30 Friday

3rd ♊
☽ enters ♋ 8:55 am
Color: White

Birthday of Oberon Zell,
Church of All Worlds

Father Urbain Grandier imprisoned in
France for bewitching nuns, 1633

The Wealthy Bull Moon

Domesticated since the early Neolithic era, owning cattle has meant wealth and power in cultures worldwide. As the leader of the herd, embodying virile strength and fertility, the bull is the epitome of abundance. The rune, Fehu (ᚠ), means cattle and brings through the energy of money, possessions, and the energy that leads to wealth.

Work toward wealth for yourself and your family or coven on this Taurus Full Moon. Find some beautiful green paper and a gold ink pen. Cut a dollar-sized piece of paper for each person participating in the ritual. In the center of each piece of paper, write the rune, Fehu, in gold ink. Surrounding the rune, write specific desires: "money for a car," "mortgage paid off," etc. Light a gold candle and chant over your creations: *Fay-who, fay-who, fay-who, reward my efforts and bless me with wealth*. Keep the paper in your wallet. Each time you open your wallet, call the chant to mind and renew the energy. Alternatively, create a money magnet by placing the paper in an envelope in a special place. Each time money comes to you, put a little into the envelope. Don't remove any unless it is for a very special reason.

—Kristin Madden

1 Saturday

3rd ♋
Color: Blue

Birthday of Anodea Judith,
president, Church of All Worlds

2 Sunday

3rd ♋
☽ v/c 1:55 am
☽ enters ♌ 8:57 pm
Color: Yellow

December

3 Monday

3rd ♌
Color: Silver

*Noon is the peak of solar magic each day, a good
time for working active or attractive magic*

4 Tuesday

3rd ♌
♀ enters ♊ 4:05 am
☽ v/c 5:08 pm
Color: Red

5 Wednesday
3rd ♌
☽ enters ♍ 6:51 am
Color: Brown

Pope Innocent VIII reverses the
Canon Episcopi by issuing the bull
Summis Desiderantes Affectibus, removing
obstacles to Inquisitors, 1484
Death of Aleister Crowley, 1947

☾ Thursday
3rd ♍
4th quarter 10:31 am
Color: Green

Death of Jacob Sprenger, coauthor
of the *Malleus Maleficarum*, 1495
Birthday of Dion Fortune, member
of the Golden Dawn, 1890

7 Friday
4th ♍
☽ v/c 5:35 am
☽ enters ♎ 1:35 pm
Color: Pink

Set in Eastern Standard Time (EST)

8 Saturday

4th ♎︎
☽ v/c 7:37 pm
Color: Black

For gentleness and compassion, burn lemon balm incense

9 Sunday

4th ♎︎
☽ enters ♏︎ 4:51 pm
Color: Gold

Hanukkah begins

December

10 Monday

4th ♏
☿ enters ♐ 8:40 pm
Color: Lavender

11 Tuesday

4th ♏
☽ v/c 8:08 am
☽ enters ♐ 5:22 pm
Color: Red

Spells for rest, introspection, and rejuvenation work well in winter

12 Wednesday

4th ♐
Color: Yellow

𝄞 Thursday
4th ♐
☽ v/c 3:42 am
New Moon 3:42 am
♅ D 7:02 am
☽ enters ♑ 4:43 pm
Color: Turquoise

First papal bull against black magic
issued by Alexander IV, 1258

14 Friday
1st ♑
Color: Coral

A. E. Waite's tarot deck is published, with art
by Pamela Colman Smith; this deck later
became known as the Rider-Waite deck, 1910

Magical Mulled Cider

1 quart (or 1 liter) apple cider
6 orange slices, sliced to look like
   the sun
12 whole cloves
⅛ tsp. nutmeg
½ tsp. ground cinnamon
6 cinnamon sticks
Honey to taste

Toast the return of the Sun God, and the holy rebirth, with this warming drink when you gather with friends and family on the longest night of the year. Best made over an open fire, but easily concocted on a stove indoors, magical mulled cider will warm the hearth, heart, and home. Sip this and know that anything is possible.

In a large pot combine apple cider which represents the virgin Goddess, orange slices which represent the Sun God, cloves, nutmeg, and ground cinnamon. Simmer for at least half an hour to make your house smell wonderfully festive, or longer for a stronger mulled taste. This simmering symbolically brings the God and Goddess together and adds a little "spice" to the mix. Pour into a mug, carefully ladling an orange slice into each cup. Add a cinnamon stick and serve. Makes 6 servings.

—Dallas Jennifer Cobb

15 Saturday
1st ♑
☽ v/c 4:15 pm
☽ enters ♒ 4:53 pm
♀ enters ♐ 11:38 pm
Color: Brown

*Golden beryl enhances psychic powers and
grants resistance against unwanted influences*

16 Sunday
1st ♒
Color: Amber

Hanukkah ends

December

17 Monday
1st ≈
☽ v/c 1:12 pm
☽ enters ♓ 7:48 pm
Color: White

Alexandrite aligns the mental, emotional, and physical bodies

18 Tuesday
1st ♓
⛢ enters ♑ 10:26 pm
Color: Black

19 Wednesday
1st ♓
Color: Topaz

Once you start making your bed,
finish the task; interruption could cause insomnia

◐ Thursday
1st ♓
☽ v/c 12:19 am
2nd quarter 12:19 am
☽ enters ♈ 2:43 am
Color: Green

21 Friday
2nd ♈
☉ enters ♑ 6:12 am
Color: Purple

Yule/Winter Solstice
Sun enters Capricorn
Janet and Stewart Farrar begin their first coven together, 1970

Set in Eastern Standard Time (EST)

Winter Solstice

The Winter Solstice marks the shortest day and the longest night, but it is never a time for despair. In the point of greatest darkness lies the spark of rebirth. Many cultures mark the longest night in a sacred way, for they understand that from this point forward, the sun's light once again begins to grow.

The Winter Solstice is a time for gathering in and settling into our inner selves for the long winter. It is an excellent time for reflection and practicing being in stillness. We can undertake rituals and meditations to honor the sacred quality of the Cosmic Darkness, which carries all the energies of life, light, and magical potential.

Create a Winter Solstice altar and decorate it with evergreen boughs, red fruits and berries like holly or pomegranate, and a cauldron full of mulled wine or fruit juice mixed with herbs for the Gods. At dusk on the solstice, extinguish all lights and let yourself sit in the sacred darkness. You may wish to sing or chant, honoring the sacred life energies which are present in the cosmic darkness. When you have concluded your work and feel the presence of spirit, light a white or gold candle and feel yourself transformed!

—Sharynne MacLeod NicMhacha

---

22 Saturday
2nd ♈
☽ v/c 7:57 am
☽ enters ♉ 1:25 pm
Color: Blue

Celtic Tree Month of Elder ends

---

23 Sunday
2nd ♉
Color: Orange

Between (Celtic Tree Month)

December

24 Monday
2nd ♉
Color: Gray

Christmas Eve
Celtic Tree Month of Birch begins

25 Tuesday
2nd ♉
☽ v/c 12:58 am
☽ enters ♊ 2:13 am
♂ enters ♒ 7:49 pm
Color: Maroon

Christmas Day
Feast of Frau Holle, Germanic weather goddess
who was believed to travel through
the world to watch people's deeds;
she blessed the good and punished the bad

26 Wednesday
2nd ♊
Color: Brown

Kwanzaa begins
Dr. Fian arraigned for twenty counts
of witchcraft and treason, 1590

27 Thursday
2nd ♊
☽ v/c 1:50 am
☽ enters ♋ 3:06 pm
Color: Crimson

Birthday of Gerina Dunwich,
Wiccan author

☺ Friday
2nd ♋
Full Moon 5:21 am
☽ v/c 9:43 am
Color: Pink

Long Nights Moon

Set in Eastern Standard Time (EST)

The Reconnecting Reindeer Moon

The modern representation of an old shaman is said to have traveled with the help of eight tiny reindeer... or was that nine with Rudolph? Reindeer have light-brown fur that turns white in the winter. They instinctively know to eat lichens and mosses containing a compound that acts as an antifreeze for their cells. These animals are completely in tune with their environment.

On this Full Moon, reconnect with the natural world. As an individual or with a group, take a walk in as undisturbed an area as possible. As you enter, offer a prayer of thanks. Breathe deeply and allow your awareness to expand. Focus on your hearing. Close your eyes and listen to all you can hear. Next, focus on your sense of touch. Feel the trees, the rocks, the dirt. Next, focus on smell and taste. Sniff the air, the land; open your mouth to taste the wind. Then, focus on your sight. Look with the eyes of someone who is in tune with the natural world. Open all five senses to the landscape and simply wander, following your attractions by approaching objects and spaces that call to you. Don't think, just be with each space and feel your connections to All That Is.

—Kristin Madden

29 Saturday
3rd ♋
Color: Gray

Reindeer as a totem enhances communication, social skills, and family ties; this is helpful for facilitators

30 Sunday
3rd ♋
☽ enters ♌ 2:45 am
Color: Orange

December/January

31 Monday
3rd ♌
☿ enters ♑ 9:03 am
☽ v/c 4:52 pm
Color: Ivory

New Year's Eve

1 Tuesday
3rd ♌
☽ enters ♍ 12:35 pm
Color: Red

New Year's Day
Kwanzaa ends

2 Wednesday
3rd ♍
Color: Brown

3 Thursday
3rd ♍
☽ v/c 7:15 am
☽ enters ♎ 8:11 pm
Color: Purple

*The Aztec goddess of marriage and prostitution is
Xochiquetzal, whose name means "flower feather"*

4 Friday
3rd ♎
4th quarter 10:58 pm
Color: White

Tuck a swan's feather in your partner's pillow to encourage fidelity

Set in Eastern Standard Time (EST)

Endings & Beginnings

To make room for the new, we must let go of the old. This is hard, even when you desire change. This spell can help you let go and start anew.

Dim the room lights, pour some pure water into a bowl, and place a white candle behind it to reflect light onto the water. Take some deep grounding breaths, light the candle, and visualize the things you are letting go of. Gently swish your hands in the water to release them. Then visualize what you wish to bring into your life and say the spell. Afterward, look into the light reflected in the bowl. Can you see the future? Isn't it bright?

I wash my hands of what once was
To make room for the future
Clearing off the past because
The present I would nurture
The old is out, the new is in
Shining bright before me
I open wide and so begin
Endless possibility

—Deborah Blake

5 Saturday
4th ♎
☽ v/c 6:13 pm
Color: Gray

Your birthday is a personal milestone;
use it to consider the year's
accomplishments and make new plans

6 Sunday
1st ♎
☽ enters ♏ 1:09 am
Color: Gold

About the Authors

ELIZABETH BARRETTE was the managing editor of *PanGaia* and has been involved with the Pagan community for twenty years, actively networking via coffeehouse meetings and open sabbats. Her other writings include speculative fiction and gender studies. Her 2005 poem "The Poltergeist of Polaris" earned a nomination for the Rhysling Award. She lives in central Illinois and enjoys herbal landscaping and gardening for wildlife.

DEBORAH BLAKE is a Wiccan High Priestess who has been leading her group, Blue Moon Circle, for nearly five years. She is the author of *Circle, Coven & Grove: A Year of Magickal Practice* and *Everyday Witch A to Z*. When not writing, Deborah runs the Artisans' Guild and works as a jewelry maker, tarot reader, ordained minister, and intuitive energy healer. She lives in a 100-year-old farmhouse in upstate New York.

Arizona author TABITHA BRADLEY is the author of eight books including *The Misadventures of Alex T'Kayn*, *Treasure Hunter*, and *Peacekeeper* as well as several articles for *Llewellyn's Magical Almanac* and *Witches' Calendar*. Tabitha is also a freelance book editor and professional digital artist. Her artistic work has been featured on the covers of her Dirandan Chronicles series for Renaissance. For a full gallery of her work, visit her blog, Diranda Studios, www.diranda.com.

DALLAS JENNIFER COBB cultivates gratitude, prosperity, and peace. Believing that "life is what you make it," she has made a magical life in a waterfront village on the shores of great Lake Ontario. She teaches Pilates, works in a library, and writes to finance long hours spent following her heart's desire—time with family, in nature, and on the water. Contact her at jennifer.cobb@live.com.

ELLEN DUGAN, the "Garden Witch," is a psychic-clairvoyant and a practicing Witch of twenty years. Ellen is a master gardener who teaches flower folklore and gardening at a community college and is the author of several Llewellyn books, including *Garden Witchery*, *Elements of Witchcraft*, *Book of Witchery*, *The Enchanted Cat*, *Herb Magic for Beginners*, and *Natural Witchery*. Ellen and her family live in Missouri.

SYBIL FOGG has been a practicing witch for over twenty years. She is also known as Sybil Wilen. She chose to use her mother's maiden name in pagan circles to honor her grandparents. She's also a wife, mother, writer, teacher, and belly dancer. Her family shares her passion for magic, dance, and writing. She lives in South Portland, Maine, with her husband and their plethora of children. Please visit her website: www.sybilwilen.com.

JENNIFER HEWITSON has been a freelance illustrator since 1985. Her illustrations have appeared in local and national publications, including the *Wall Street Journal*, the *Washington Post*, the *Los Angeles Times*, *US News & World Report*, and *Ladybug* magazine. Her advertising and packaging clients include Disney and the San Diego Zoo. Jennifer has created a line of greeting cards for Sun Rise Publications, and has illustrated several children's books. Her work has been recognized by numerous organizations, including the Society of Illustrators Los Angeles, and magazines such as *Communication Arts*, *Print*, and *How*.

JAMES KAMBOS holds a degree in history and geography from Ohio University. Born and raised in Appalachia of and Greek ancestry, James learned the folk magic ways of Appalachia and the Near East at an early age. He writes, paints, and gardens from his home in Ohio.

SHARYNNE MACLEOD NICMHACHA is a Celtic teacher, writer, and bard of Scottish, Irish, and Welsh ancestry, and a direct descendant of "Fairy Clan" MacLeod. She trained in Celtic Studies through Harvard University, and has presented and published work in North America, Ireland, and Scotland. Sharynne serves as faculty in Celtic Pagan religion and shamanism at Omega, Kripalu, and Rowe, and at the Celtic Institute of North America. She is also a professional singer and musician, and an aspiring ban-fili (Celtic poet-seer). www.mobiusbandwidth.com/dns.html.

KRISTIN MADDEN is the author of ten books, including *Shamanic Guide to Death and Dying*, *The Book of Shamanic Healing*, and the 2009 COVR Visionary Award finalist *Magick, Mystery, and Medicine*. Raised in a shamanic home, Kristin has had ongoing experience with both Eastern and Western mystic paths since 1972. She also runs a wildlife rehabilitation clinic, trains educational raptors, and works as a field biologist.

Appendix

Daily Magical Influences

Each day is ruled by a planet with specific magical influences.

Monday (Moon): peace, healing, caring, psychic awareness
Tuesday (Mars): passion, courage, aggression, protection
Wednesday (Mercury): study, travel, divination, wisdom
Thursday (Jupiter): expansion, money, prosperity, generosity
Friday (Venus): love, friendship, reconciliation, beauty
Saturday (Saturn): longevity, endings, homes
Sunday (Sun): healing, spirituality, success, strength, protection

Color Correspondences

Colors are associated with each day, according to planetary influence.

Monday: gray, lavender, white, silver, ivory
Tuesday: red, white, black, gray, maroon, scarlet
Wednesday: yellow, brown, white, topaz
Thursday: green, turquoise, white, purple, crimson
Friday: white, pink, rose, purple, coral
Saturday: brown, gray, blue, indigo, black
Sunday: yellow, orange, gold, amber

Lunar Phases

Waxing, from New Moon to Full Moon, is the ideal time to do magic to draw things to you.

Waning, from Full Moon to New Moon, is a time for study, meditation, and magical work designed to banish harmful energies.

The Moon's Sign

The Moon continuously moves through each sign of the zodiac, from Aries to Pisces, staying about two and a half days in each sign. The Moon influences the sign it inhabits, creating different energies that affect our day-to-day lives.

Aries: Good for starting things. Things occur rapidly, but quickly pass. People tend to be argumentative and assertive.

Taurus: Things begun now last longest, tend to increase in value, and become hard to change. Brings out an appreciation for beauty and sensory experience.

Gemini: Things begun now are easily changed by outside influence. Time for shortcuts, communication, games, and fun.

Cancer: Stimulates emotional rapport between people. Supports growth and nurturing. Tend to domestic concerns.

Leo: Draws emphasis to the self, to central ideas or institutions, away from connections with others and emotional needs.

Virgo: Favors accomplishment of details and commands from higher up. Focus on health, hygiene, and daily schedules.

Libra: Favors cooperation, compromise, social activities, balance, friendship, and partnership.

Scorpio: Increases awareness of psychic power. Precipitates psychic crises and ends connections thoroughly. People have a tendency to brood and become secretive.

Sagittarius: Encourages confidence and flights of imagination. This is an adventurous, philosophical, and athletic Moon sign. Favors expansion and growth.

Capricorn: Develops strong structure. Focus on traditions, responsibilities, and obligations. A good time to set boundaries and rules.

Aquarius: Rebellious energy. Time to break habits and make abrupt change. Personal freedom and individuality is the focus.

Pisces: The focus is on dreaming, nostalgia, intuition, and psychic impressions. A good time for spiritual or philanthropic activities.

2012 Eclipses

May 20, 7:23 pm; Solar eclipse 0° ♊ 21'
June 4, 7:03 am; Lunar eclipse 14° ♐ 08'
November 13, 5:17 pm; Solar eclipse 21° ♏ 57'
November 28, 9:33 am; Lunar eclipse 6° ♊ 40'

2012 Full Moons

Cold Moon: January 9, 2:30 am
Quickening Moon: February 7, 4:54 pm
Storm Moon: March 8, 4:39 am
Wind Moon: April 6, 3:19 pm
Flower Moon: May 5, 11:35 pm
Strong Sun Moon: June 4, 7:12 am
Blessing Moon: July 3, 2:52 pm
Corn Moon: August 1, 11:27 pm
Blue Moon: August 31, 9:58 am
Harvest Moon: September 29, 11:19 pm
Blood Moon: October 29, 3:49 pm
Mourning Moon: November 28, 9:46 am
Long Nights Moon: December 28, 5:21 am

Planetary Retrogrades in 2012

Mars	℞	01/23/12	7:54 pm	— Direct	04/13/12	11:53 pm
Saturn	℞	02/07/12	9:03 am	— Direct	06/25/12	4:00 am
Mercury	℞	03/12/12	3:49 am	— Direct	04/04/12	6:11 am
Pluto	℞	04/10/12	12:21 pm	— Direct	09/18/12	1:07 am
Venus	℞	05/15/12	10:33 am	— Direct	06/27/12	11:07 am
Neptune	℞	06/04/12	5:03 pm	— Direct	11/11/12	2:52 am
Uranus	℞	07/13/12	5:49 am	— Direct	12/13/12	7:02 am
Mercury	℞	07/14/12	10:16 pm	— Direct	08/08/12	1:40 am
Jupiter	℞	10/04/12	9:18 am	— Direct	01/30/13	6:37 am
Mercury	℞	11/06/12	6:04 pm	— Direct	11/26/12	5:48 pm

Set in Eastern Time. All times corrected for Daylight Saving Time.

Moon Void-of-Course Data for 2012

Last Aspect		New Sign	
Date	Time	Sign	New Time

JANUARY

Date	Time	Sign	New Time
2	3:07 pm	2 ♉	5:16 pm
5	3:46 am	5 ♊	5:44 am
7	2:52 pm	7 ♋	4:05 pm
9	9:25 pm	9 ♌	11:35 pm
12	3:23 am	12 ♍	4:44 pm
13	8:58 pm	14 ♎	8:28 am
16	10:29 am	16 ♏	11:33 pm
18	1:31 pm	18 ♐	2:29 pm
20	4:49 pm	20 ♑	5:40 pm
22	8:38 pm	22 ♒	9:53 pm
25	3:33 am	25 ♓	4:11 am
26	11:53 pm	27 ♈	1:28 pm
30	1:08 am	30 ♉	1:28 pm

FEBRUARY

Date	Time	Sign	New Time
1	2:06 pm	1 ♊	2:14 pm
4	12:06 am	4 ♋	1:04 am
6	7:31 am	6 ♌	8:24 am
8	11:42 am	8 ♍	12:32 pm
10	12:11 am	10 ♎	2:54 pm
12	4:09 pm	12 ♏	5:01 pm
14	12:04 am	14 ♐	7:56 pm
16	11:03 pm	17 ♑	12:03 am
19	4:22 am	19 ♒	5:28 am
21	11:17 am	21 ♓	12:31 pm
22	9:24 pm	23 ♈	9:48 pm
26	7:52 am	26 ♉	9:29 am
28	2:46 pm	28 ♊	10:27 pm

MARCH

Date	Time	Sign	New Time
2	8:14 am	2 ♋	10:08 am
4	5:17 pm	4 ♌	6:17 pm
6	8:27 pm	6 ♍	10:27 pm
8	4:39 am	8 ♎	11:50 pm
10	10:09 am	11 ♏	12:24 am
12	2:30 pm	13 ♐	2:54 am
15	3:34 am	15 ♑	6:24 am
17	9:00 am	17 ♒	12:11 pm
19	4:31 pm	19 ♓	8:05 pm
21	4:39 am	22 ♈	5:57 am
24	1:17 pm	24 ♉	5:43 pm
27	12:35 am	27 ♊	6:43 am
29	2:05 pm	29 ♋	7:07 pm

APRIL

Date	Time	Sign	New Time
1	12:20 am	1 ♌	4:35 am
3	9:47 am	3 ♍	9:53 am
5	1:37 am	5 ♎	11:32 am
7	6:15 am	7 ♏	11:18 am
9	2:56 am	9 ♐	11:12 am
11	7:06 am	11 ♑	1:02 pm
13	1:05 pm	13 ♒	5:48 pm
15	6:42 pm	16 ♓	1:38 am
17	10:34 am	18 ♈	11:59 am
20	3:35 pm	21 ♉	12:05 am
22	1:10 pm	23 ♊	1:05 pm
25	4:31 pm	26 ♋	1:42 am
28	3:05 am	28 ♌	12:10 pm
30	10:17 am	30 ♍	7:02 pm

MAY

Date	Time	Sign	New Time
2	6:58 am	2 ♎	10:04 pm
4	2:02 pm	5 ♏	10:20 pm
6	8:14 am	6 ♐	9:39 pm
8	9:34 am	8 ♑	10:00 pm
10	3:11 pm	11 ♒	1:03 am
12	8:52 pm	13 ♓	7:42 am
15	7:59 am	15 ♈	5:45 pm
17	5:44 pm	18 ♉	6:03 am
20	8:35 am	20 ♊	7:05 pm
22	6:51 pm	23 ♋	7:31 am
25	10:34 am	25 ♌	6:11 pm
27	7:54 pm	28 ♍	2:06 am
30	1:50 am	30 ♎	6:46 am
31	9:31 pm	6/1 ♏	8:31 am

JUNE

Date	Time	Sign	New Time
5/31	9:31 pm	1 ♏	8:31 am
3	5:29 am	3 ♐	8:32 am
5	1:08 am	5 ♑	8:31 am
7	8:38 am	7 ♒	10:17 am
9	2:33 pm	9 ♓	3:22 pm
11	6:41 am	12 ♈	12:21 am
13	11:09 pm	14 ♉	12:22 pm
16	8:09 am	17 ♊	1:24 am
19	11:02 am	19 ♋	1:34 pm
21	12:48 pm	21 ♌	11:47 pm
23	6:26 pm	24 ♍	7:42 am
26	6:53 am	26 ♎	1:15 pm
28	4:22 am	28 ♏	4:32 pm
30	3:46 pm	30 ♐	6:04 pm

JULY

Date	Time	Sign	New Time
2	6:21 pm	2 ♑	6:51 pm
4	8:25 am	4 ♒	8:26 pm
6	11:49 am	7 ♓	12:29 am
8	7:00 am	9 ♈	8:14 am
11	5:23 am	11 ♉	7:30 pm
13	3:46 pm	14 ♊	8:26 am
16	6:56 am	16 ♋	8:31 pm
19	12:24 am	19 ♌	6:13 am
21	1:17 pm	21 ♍	1:24 pm
22	8:44 pm	23 ♎	6:38 pm
25	11:22 am	25 ♏	10:29 pm
26	11:38 am	28 ♐	1:18 am
29	5:01 pm	30 ♑	3:29 am
31	7:30 pm	8/1 ♒	5:56 am

AUGUST

Date	Time	Sign	New Time
7/31	7:30 pm	1 ♒	5:56 am
3	3:24 am	3 ♓	9:58 am
5	1:56 am	5 ♈	4:59 pm
7	4:04 pm	8 ♉	3:28 am
9	2:55 pm	10 ♊	4:11 pm
12	5:49 am	13 ♋	4:27 am
15	4:21 am	15 ♌	2:05 pm
17	1:55 pm	17 ♍	8:33 pm
18	7:26 pm	20 ♎	12:45 am
22	3:13 am	22 ♏	3:54 am
23	5:34 am	24 ♐	6:50 am
26	2:39 am	26 ♑	9:58 am
28	6:33 am	28 ♒	1:38 pm
30	1:48 pm	30 ♓	6:31 pm

SEPTEMBER

Date	Time	Sign	New Time
1	4:02 pm	2 ♈	1:37 am
4	7:06 am	4 ♉	11:41 am
5	2:54 pm	7 ♊	12:10 am
9	6:59 am	9 ♋	12:49 pm
11	5:58 pm	11 ♌	11:00 pm
14	1:14 am	14 ♍	5:30 am
16	7:26 am	16 ♎	8:55 am
18	7:30 am	18 ♏	10:46 am
20	9:11 am	20 ♐	12:34 pm
22	12:45 pm	22 ♑	3:20 pm
24	5:19 pm	24 ♒	7:32 pm
26	11:33 pm	27 ♓	1:23 am
28	10:35 pm	29 ♈	9:14 am

OCTOBER

Date	Time	Sign	New Time
1	6:32 pm	1 ♉	7:26 pm
4	3:44 am	4 ♊	7:47 am
5	5:08 pm	6 ♋	8:45 pm
8	3:33 am	9 ♌	7:55 am
10	5:40 pm	11 ♍	3:23 pm
12	7:48 pm	13 ♎	7:02 pm
15	8:02 am	15 ♏	8:06 pm
16	10:23 pm	17 ♐	8:26 pm
19	4:27 pm	19 ♑	9:41 pm
21	11:32 pm	22 ♒	1:02 am
23	9:27 pm	24 ♓	7:00 am
26	11:04 pm	26 ♈	3:31 pm
27	9:32 pm	29 ♉	2:15 am
29	5:01 pm	31 ♊	2:40 pm

NOVEMBER

Date	Time	Sign	New Time
2	5:21 am	3 ♋	3:43 am
4	3:37 am	5 ♌	2:39 pm
7	10:27 am	7 ♍	11:35 pm
9	7:27 pm	10 ♎	6:10 am
12	12:13 am	12 ♏	6:10 am
14	5:39 am	14 ♐	5:52 am
16	4:44 am	16 ♑	5:35 am
18	12:54 am	18 ♒	7:10 am
20	9:31 am	20 ♓	11:55 am
22	1:32 pm	22 ♈	8:12 pm
23	8:34 pm	25 ♉	7:18 am
26	7:57 pm	27 ♊	7:58 pm
28	8:04 pm	30 ♋	8:55 am

DECEMBER

Date	Time	Sign	New Time
2	1:55 am	2 ♌	8:57 pm
4	5:08 pm	5 ♍	6:51 am
7	5:35 am	7 ♎	1:35 pm
8	7:37 pm	9 ♏	4:51 pm
11	8:08 am	11 ♐	5:22 pm
13	3:42 am	13 ♑	4:43 pm
15	4:15 pm	15 ♒	4:53 pm
17	1:12 pm	17 ♓	7:48 pm
20	12:19 am	20 ♈	2:43 am
22	7:57 am	22 ♉	1:25 pm
25	12:58 am	25 ♊	2:13 am
27	1:50 am	27 ♋	3:06 pm
28	9:43 am	30 ♌	2:45 am
31	4:52 pm	1/1 ♍	12:35 pm

Notes

Notes

Notes